MW01701371

LIFE IS A MEETING

LIFE IS A MEETING

CHUCK DOWDLE

BookWork
STUDIO

Life Is a Meeting

Printed in the United States of America

BookWork Studio
442 Charnelton St.
Eugene, OR 97401

LCCN: 2024923401
ISBN: 979-8-88679-717-6

This play is dedicated to Marty Dowdle,
Carmelle Matthes Dowdle and Allie LeCaux,
without whom it would never have seen the light of day.
Thank you to the three of you.
I love you all very much and always will.

List of Characters Page

MAIN CHARACTERS:

Narrator

Marty Dowdle — Mother of fraternal twin sons, Mark and Michael

Chuck Dowdle — Father of fraternal twin sons, Mark and Michael

Mark Dowdle — Son of Marty and Chuck Dowdle

Michael Dowdle — Son of Marty and Chuck Dowdle

Grace Johnson — Mother of identical twin daughters, Laurie and Linda

Walter Johnson — Father of identical twin daughters, Laurie and Linda

Laurie Johnson — Daughter of Grace and Walter Johnson

Linda Johnson — Daughter of Grace and Walter Johnson

Carmelle Matthes Dowdle — Second wife of Chuck Dowdle

LIFE IS A MEETING

ACT I: LEAVING HOME

Scene I: Tethered

NARRATOR: Michael and Mark Dowdle are fraternal twins born prematurely at five and a half months gestation on August 9, 1953 in Perham, Minnesota. The twins weigh one and a half pounds apiece at birth and are not expected to live, but they do! They are called the "Miracle Twins!" However, not all is a miracle. Like many other babies who are born prematurely at that time, Mark and Michael are given excess oxygen to keep them alive, and the excess oxygen causes many babies to go **blind**! That is Mark's case, and he is tethered to Michael so he won't get hurt, even when he is a baby, crawling around on the floor and playing with his brother. Time passes rapidly, and during the opening scene the twins are high school seniors getting ready to graduate, so they're not crawling around anymore. Now they're sprinting around the Perham High School track, still tethered, and talking about the speeches they're going to be giving. The twins carry straight "A" averages during their high school careers, and the administration is in a quandary about its choice for a valedictorian. It solves the problem by simply making them co-valedictorians.

(The scene opens with Michael breathing hard and gasping.)

Michael: Damn, Brother! If you keep developing your athleticism on the track any more than you already have, you'll soon be leading me instead of me leading you!

Mark: That'll be the day! But it was a nice thought, Michael.

(The twins take one last lap and sprint for the finish line before quitting their workout for the day.)

Michael: Have you finished writing your graduation speech yet?

Mark: Not yet, but I'm getting there. It's sort of difficult to know what to say. I'm still thinking on it, but I'm getting there. How about you?

Michael: I'm done with mine. Now I'm just going over it so I don't screw up on graduation day. It isn't going to be easy seeing all of our fellow students and their parents staring at us, waiting to hear what we're going to say.

Mark: I won't have any trouble with that, Michael. I won't see a thing!

(Both boys have a good laugh as they walk towards the gym, still talking about their graduation speeches.)

Scene II: Graduation

NARRATOR: It's a beautiful June day. The sun is shining down on more than one hundred graduates-to-be, all seated on folding chairs on the football field and facing an elevated stage. Seated behind the students are rows of relatives and friends, all there to celebrate the moment when their loved ones will be declared bona fide graduates of Perham High School. After the band performs a rousing welcome and a few requisite introductions are given, Mark rises slowly, cane in hand, and taps his way across the wooden stage floor to the podium.

Mark: Good afternoon, ladies and gentlemen. It's wonderful to have all of you here to recognize and celebrate our Perham High School graduating class of 1970. My name, for those of you who don't know me, is Mark Dowdle, and it's my pleasure this afternoon to say a few words, along with my twin brother Michael in honor of this momentous occasion.

(A hush falls over the audience as Mark stands silent for a long time and gazes out as if he's seeing, but his hands are moving rapidly on his braille sheets on the podium. Then, finally, he continues speaking, and everyone breathes a sigh of relief.)

Mark: Parents, teachers, friends and classmates, the time has come to say farewell, and I say to my fellow students and graduates-to-be, shoot for the moon! We've certainly been living during extraordinary times, have we not? Who would have thought that in 1968 the Apollo 8 astronauts would be flying ten orbits around the moon, that in 1969 the Apollo II, with 12 astronauts, would be landing on the moon! They collected samples, took photographs, and set up experiments, all from 239,000 miles away! It may be that none of us end up on a flight to the moon, but we have plenty of excitement ahead of us. The world is ours to explore! Living lives of continued learning and adventure are ours to pursue! We all have good reason to be inspired by anticipating what lies ahead! Do you agree?

(Students yelling "Yes! Yes! Yes!")

Mark: That loud response I just heard tells me you do!

(Mark pauses for a few moments and waits for the crowd to quiet down, and then he looks out as if he's able to see and continues speaking.)

Mark: Did you know that even though the moon is the brightest object in the night sky, it doesn't give off any light of its own? It's only reflecting light from the sun? That's how I see us as we leave here and embark on our new paths. We are reflectors of light. We've gone through many phases of life since starting our schooling, and we've been fortunate to have our parents, teachers and friends encourage and support us along the way. Now it's our turn to stand proud, help ourselves and prepare to help others! My brother Michael and I intend to do just that when we enter St. John's University at Collegeville in the fall. Michael will be studying to be a medical doctor and I'll be studying law. It doesn't matter what career you choose as long as you're happy doing it. Whatever your work, make sure you feel passionate about it because it will be a major chapter in your life. I'd like to close by reciting the beginning of one of my favorite stories from the Bible. It's about a man who was born blind, and Jesus helped him see:

And as He was passing by, He saw a man blind from birth. And His disciples asked Him: "Rabbi, who has sinned, this man or his parents, that he should be born blind?" Jesus answered: "Neither has this man sinned, nor his parents, but the works of God were to be made manifest to him. I must do the works of Him who sent me while it is day; night is coming when no one can work. As long as I am in the world, I am the light of the world."

(Silence is all that can be heard, briefly, and then the applause starts, and it roars, and Mark's fellow graduates yell wildly and a big smile fills his face. He waits for the noise to die down and then continues enthusiastically.)

Mark: So, there you have it, my friends! Shoot for the moon! Reflect your bright light wherever you go! Thank you for the love and kindness you've shown me over the years. I will always remember you and the inspiring and supportive teachers who were an integral part of my high school experience. Lastly, I'm especially grateful for my parents and my brother Michael. They have been my eyes, my heart, and truly the bright lights of my life!

(The crowd hushes, all eyes on Mark, as they begin to feel the emotional magnitude of this day with him. Mark pauses to compose himself.)

Mark: I'll turn the microphone over to Michael now so he can share a few words of wisdom with you.

(The audience cheers and applauds as Michael approaches

Mark, and it continues as the two brothers exchange a warm embrace. Then Michael puts his arm around his brother's shoulder and guides him back to his seat before approaching the podium himself and beginning his address.)

Michael: I don't know about wisdom, but thank you for your kind words, Mark. And thank you for sharing your wisdom with all of us. Over the past 17 years I've learned so much from you about kindness, tolerance, respect, generosity…the list goes on. Needless to say, I feel exceedingly blessed to have you as my brother. To you Mark, to our parents, teachers, classmates and friends here today, whatever wisdom I may have is thanks to all of you. Each of you in your own way has helped me to be successful throughout this high school journey, and like my brother, I couldn't have done it without your love and support. I'm sure all of my fellow seniors sitting out there feel the same way about their teachers, friends and families, filled with gratitude for those who've impacted their schooling and lives in such a positive way. It's difficult to say goodbye, but this chapter now ends, and it's time to turn the page and start writing the next one! We did it! It's time to spread our wings and fly!

(Michael stands smiling at the students as they cheer and applaud, and then continues.)

Michael: What it all means is that we're going to be making some serious choices for our futures, including decisions about college and careers. Mark and I are lucky, as it was pretty easy for us to narrow down the options. I knew from a young age that I wanted to be a medical doctor, and Mark decided he was interested in

becoming a lawyer. Choosing a college was pretty easy for both of us as well. We'll be attending St. John's University, our dad's alma mater.

Some of you may find it challenging to choose a path to follow. That's okay! It's okay to be uncertain! Yesterday, you were high school students; today you'll become high school graduates! Take some time to kindle your passions and discover what it is that most speaks to your heart! Never give up, no matter how difficult the road ahead may seem. All that matters is that you feel good about what you're doing or what you're studying, and that you take it on with determination and courage and 100% effort. If you do that, everything will fall into place, and you will succeed!

(Michael pauses and gazes out at the rows of smiling faces.)

Michael: My friends, I know I began by telling you I don't know about wisdom, but when I recall the inspirational words of my mother, I'm reminded that I carry with me her words of wisdom: **When a job is once begun, be the labor great or small, never leave it 'til it's done, do it well or not at all!** My mother's words have as much truth for us today as they did for her many years ago, true and simple words of wisdom. And so, with that, I bid you farewell, my friends! May your futures be filled with peace and happiness! Now let's get on with this show and graduate!

(The whole audience stands and applauds exuberantly, and the graduates yell and whistle until Michael turns and walks to his chair and is seated. The principal approaches the podium, the graduates receive their diplomas, the band plays, mortarboards go sailing high into the air, and the Perham High School class of 1970 is officially set free!)

Scene III: Summer

NARRATOR: Marty, the boys' mom, prepares a delicious graduation supper for her sons, and as the scene opens, the family is holding hands, and Chuck, the boys' dad, begins the meal with a prayer.

Chuck: *Lord, thank you for letting our sons live! Thank you for guiding them and helping them succeed with their education. And thank you for letting us be a vital part of their lives.* We *praise you, Lord, and ask that you remain with them. Amen.*

(Everyone begins eating the walleyed pike Chuck caught early that morning at Big Pine Lake and Marty fried to a crispy golden brown with potatoes.)

Mark: Man, this is delicious, Mom! You sure know how to fix fish!

Marty: Well, I've had a lot of experience, Mark.

Chuck: Hey! How about me? I got up early this morning and caught them!

Michael: Yeah, we know, Dad, but Mom's got that touch that makes them so good to eat!

Chuck: Don't expect St. John's to be easy when you get there, you two, because it won't be. I worked my butt off just to survive! And you both received scholarships, so a lot will be expected of you.

Michael: You worry too much, Dad. We'll be fine.

Mark: Yeah, Dad, take it easy. We're your brilliant offspring! Remember?

Chuck: (laughing) Okay, okay. I'm just glad I'm not you, Michael! All those science classes!

Michael: That's the best part, Dad. Biology and chemistry! I can hardly wait! That's why I'm taking pre-med.

(Marty just sits quietly and takes it all in because she knows Chuck and her sons like to banter back and forth.)

Mark: (seriously) Mom, we're really going to miss your cooking. And we're going to miss you and Dad.

Marty: It will be way too quiet around here. I know you two will do just fine away at college, and Chuck and I are excited for both of you, but we sure will miss you!

NARRATOR: The summer passes quickly. A lot of goodbyes are said to their friends and fellow students, and the Saturday before the twins leave for St. John's, Michael hears a knock on the door.

When he opens it, he is surprised to see Tom Schmitz, the Perham Ford dealer and a fellow Johnnie of his dad's, standing there.)

Tom: (enthusiastically) Hi, Michael! Tell your mom and dad their new car is sitting outside!

Michael: (confused) New car?

Tom: Didn't they tell you? They're giving you two boys the old car to take to St. John's, and they bought a new one for themselves. (Tom points to a shiny four-door silver sedan sitting by the curb.) There she sits!

Michael: (excited) Wow! That's great news for all of us!

Chuck: (approaching the door and laughing) Well, I guess the cat came flying out of that bag!

Tom: (apologetically) I'm afraid it did, Charlie. I'm sorry about that. I thought the boys knew.

Chuck: That's okay, Tom. We were getting ready to tell them, anyway. Now is as good a time as any.

> (Mark joins his brother and dad at the door to find out what's going on. When he hears Michael and he are going to have the old family car to take to St. John's, he erupts with joy.)

Mark: Wow! What a great surprise! Thanks, Dad!

Michael: (gushing as Chuck hands him the keys to the old car) Yeah! Thanks, Dad!

Now we're really going to have fun at college, Mark!

Scene IV: On the Road

NARRATOR: Near the end of August, the college-bound twins are driving south on Highway 78 in the family's old fire-hydrant-red Ford Country Sedan. They don't get more than a few miles out of town and are driving alongside beautiful Otter Tail Lake when Mark feels a sudden bump.

Mark: What was that?

Michael: (unconcerned as he drives happily down the highway) What was what?

Mark: Didn't you feel it? Something's going on with the car in the front on my side. I think we'd better stop and check it out.

Michael: I think you're worried about nothing, but I'll take a look just to make sure.

(Michael pulls over and gets out of the car.)

Michael: (yelling) Damn! We've got a flat!

(Michael moves quickly, unloading their suitcases so he can get to the spare tire. It takes some time and a little doing, but within an hour they're ready to roll. A sweaty Michael hops back into the driver's seat and eases the station wagon back onto the highway.)

Michael: Well, no more tires to spare. Hopefully that won't happen again!

(The miles roll by, and the boys soon find themselves driving off the main highway and onto the blacktop road leading to St. John's University.)

Mark: I can't believe we're actually at the university.

Michael: It's beautiful, Mark! There are trees all along the road and walkways and the red brick buildings look old like they've been here forever.

Mark: I'm glad we're finally here, Michael. That means we'll soon be settled in our dorm room and sitting down for our first Johnnie meal. I'm hungry!

(The boys unpack and hear bells ringing shortly after moving into their dorm in St. Mary's Hall.)

Mark: I know what that means, supper in fifteen minutes. Let's go!

ACT II:
THE MEETING

Scene I: The Refectory

NARRATOR: Michael takes Mark's hand as they leave their dorm room and walk towards the refectory. He describes the scene to his brother, students coming from all directions, black-robed monks walking towards the dining hall alongside them, and freshman students, like them, looking rather lost.

Michael: This is pretty exciting!

Mark: I'll say!

(When they arrive at the dining hall, they soon discover that it's nothing like home. Rows of students are seated on benches at long rectangular tables where monks are also seated. On the tabletops are plates, silverware, napkins, salt and pepper, thick slices of heavy dark "Johnnie Bread" and large bowls of peanut butter.)

Michael: (whispering to Mark after they're seated) There's no butter on the table, just peanut butter and heavy, dark bread, so I think we're expected to eat that with our supper.

Mark: (whispering) Are you kidding me?

(Mark no sooner gets those four words out of his mouth when silence occurs and a priest begins praying.)

Priest: *Heavenly Father, bless us as we begin a new school year, and bless this food, which has been gracefully prepared for us by the sisters. We pray, Lord, that the freshman students make a smooth adjustment to their new living arrangements and college life and that all students and faculty experience a successful school year. Amen.*

(The "Johnnie Bread" and peanut butter disappear rapidly. Michael is lucky to grab slices for Mark and himself before it's all gone.)

Michael: (whispering) This isn't going to be like home, Mark. They're now serving us smoked liver sausage, sauerkraut and boiled potatoes. How are you going to like that with your black bread and peanut butter?

Mark: (quietly) Not very well, I think, but I'll give it a try.

NARRATOR: During the next several days the twins adjust to the food, and they like the fact that their dorm room is on the first floor of St. Mary's Hall. Mark has some difficulty at first making his way from class to class, but thanks to help from his fellow Johnnies, he soon conquers the maze of pathways to his classrooms and begins feeling right at home. Michael has it easy, spending the majority of his time in the science building.

Scene II: The Mixer

NARRATOR: The most enjoyable adjustment for the twins occurs near the end of September when all the freshmen are invited to a dance at St. Benedict's College, a Catholic women's school located just a few miles from St. John's University. The dance starts at 9:00 p.m., and a caravan of "Johnnie" buses pulls up in front of St. John's at 8:30 p.m. to transport all of the eager St. John's freshmen to St. Ben's. The dance is held in the gym, where orange, yellow, brown and green foliage line the walls, and orange and black lanterns hang from the ceiling, creating an innocent but seductive feel.

Michael: (walking slowly around the dance floor with Mark and describing the décor to him) Wow! This is very interesting, Mark!

(Michael stops abruptly, causing Mark to stumble over him and almost fall.)

Mark: What's going on, Michael? You just about made me fall and make a fool of myself!

Michael: (apologetically) I'm sorry! I'm sorry! I just noticed two of the most beautiful girls I've ever seen! They have blond hair, gorgeous smiles, and are both wearing pink angora sweaters. They're about twenty feet from us, talking to each other. They look like identical twins!

Mark: (laughing) Well, don't just stand there, Michael! What are you waiting for? Let's get them out on the dance floor before a couple of studs beat us to it!

(The twins approach the co-eds.)

Michael: Hi! Would you two care to dance?

Coeds: (answering in unison and smiling) Sure! We'd love to!

Mark: You two must be twins.

Laurie: (laughing) Uh…we are. Pretty easy to tell, don't you think?

Michael: (responding quickly) Not so easy for him. This is my twin brother Mark. He's blind. I'm Michael.

Laurie: (apologetically) Oh, I'm so sorry! It's hard to tell anything in this dark gym. I'm Laurie, Laurie Johnson, and this is my twin sister Linda.

Linda: (laughing) How crazy is this! Two sets of twins meeting at a twin college "mixer!"

Mark: (waiting patiently before he can get a word in) Michael's the energetic genius; he's taking pre-med and plans on becoming a surgeon.

Michael: (smiling and putting his arm on his brother's

shoulder) And Mark's the brilliant analytic, calm and confident. He's pre-law.

Mark: How about you two?

Linda: You won't believe this, but I'm pre-law, too. We may be having some courses together because I understand St. John's and St. Ben's share classes on occasion. My sister's studying to be a nurse.

Mark: Wow, a nurse and a lawyer! That's great!

Michael: Where are you two from?

Laurie: Coon Rapids

Mark: We know where that is. We have cousins who live in Columbia Heights. Michael and I are from Perham.

(Before either of the Bennies gets a chance to respond, the music begins playing a slow number.)

Michael: Would you two like to dance now?

Laurie: We'd love to!

(Michael reaches for Laurie, and Linda takes Mark's outstretched hand in hers. Linda and Mark move gently and easily around the floor as if they've danced together for years. After dancing two slow numbers, a fast swing tune begins being played.)

Mark: Would you care if we sat this one out and had something to drink? It's getting sort of hot in here!

Linda: (warmly) Not at all, Mark!

(Linda's voice melts Mark's heart. The couple finds a table in a quiet corner.)

Linda: Laurie and I chose St. Ben's because our mother went here. Why did Michael and you choose St. John's?

Mark: Our dad graduated from St. John's, and Michael and I were lucky enough to get scholarships, so it was a pretty easy decision. So far, we love it, and being here at the dance and meeting girls like you and your sister, well, that's a dream come true! I hope we'll be able to see more of each other!

Linda: I'd love that, Mark, and I think it's safe to say Laurie would as well. Let me just tell you, she and Michael are both looking pretty happy out there on the dance floor.

(They laugh. After a few more songs, there's a break in the music, and Laurie and Michael join Linda and Mark at their table.)

Michael: (kiddingly) What are you two doing way back here?

Mark: (laughing) The music was too fast for my two left feet, plus this breather has given us a chance to find out more about each other.

(The two couples chat through another couple of fast tunes, and then a slow one begins being played.)

Michael: There's a nice slow one, Laurie. Would you like to go back out?

Laurie: (eagerly) You don't have to ask me twice, Michael. Let's go!

Linda: They seem to be genuinely enjoying each other. Would you like to try again with this slower piece?

Mark: Sure!

(They stand and Linda links her arm through Mark's as they walk to the dance floor. The evening rolls by and the happy couples continue dancing until it's time for the boys to hop on the bus and head back to St. John's. Michael can't conceal his excitement.)

Michael: (whispering emphatically to Mark) Brother, I think I'm in love!

Mark: (smiling and whispering quietly back to his brother) Well, you're not the only one! Love at first sight! And I couldn't even see Linda! But I sure could sense something special!

Michael: (laughing quietly) Those girls really got to us!

Mark: (smiling) I know! My heart felt like it was leaping out of my chest! I can hardly wait to see Linda again!

Michael: I know what you mean, Mark! I already miss Laurie!

NARRATOR: As they leave the bus and walk towards St. Mary's Hall, Michael and Mark continue talking about Laurie and Linda. Their conversation moves on to the serious studying facing them, but they can hardly wait to write home and tell their parents about the Johnnie-Bennie mixer.

Scene III: Love at First Sight

Mark: (Mark dictates a letter to his parents and has Michael write it out for him.)

September 30, 1970

Dear Mom and Dad,

We just got back to our room after a night out, and I'm writing this letter to you because something wonderful happened tonight! Michael and I went to a dance at St. Ben's, and it seems that we fell instantly in love with twin coeds from Coon Rapids! I'm not kidding! The girls' names are Laurie and Linda Johnson. Michael couldn't stop talking about Laurie on the bus ride back to St. John's, and I can't stop thinking about Linda.

She's a pre-law student just like me. We'll probably have some courses together because Bennies and Johnnies share some of their classes. How sweet that would be!

Well, it's past midnight and I have a full day of studying tomorrow, so I'd better be getting to bed. I just wanted to share our good news with you. I hope all's well back home.

— Love, Mark

NARRATOR: Monday morning arrives, reality sets in, and the twins begin attacking their studies in earnest. That doesn't mean they are thinking any less about Laurie and Linda, but they know they have to maintain a "B" or better average in all their subjects in order to retain their scholarships, and that means only one thing, work! Before the week ends, a letter arrives from their dad, and they are eager to hear what he has to say.)

Michael: (Michael reads their dad's letter out loud to Mark.)

October 6, 1970

Dear Mark and Michael,

Your mom and I got a good chuckle out of Mark's letter, telling us that you two were madly in love after meeting twin Bennies at a dance! Well, all I can say is one never knows!" You both seem to be adjusting to life at St. John's, and that's great! I still remember some of the excellent professors I had. Reverend Bonifice Axtman would say, "Well, Mr. Dowdle, it's nice of you to be with us this morning," whenever I'd walk into his philosophy class late on a Monday morning after visiting Mom over the weekend in Minneapolis. It was embarrassing, but well worth it to be able to see her. Another prof I remember well was Rev. Arno Gustin. I couldn't figure out what to write for a research paper in his Education class, and he suggested I define liberal education. Believe me, that got me thinking, and I remember my thesis was: "A liberal education is that which is most in accord with man's nature."

That was the thing about St. John's. It got me thinking more than at any other time in my life. It sure was a joy! Another joy was having Rev. Bernardo Martinez for my Principles of Economics course for two semesters. I loved the subject and got A's both semesters. Father Bernardo was a great teacher and a truly nice person.

It was a long time ago, 1952, when I graduated, but I sometimes wonder if any of the monks I remember are still teaching. I'll always remember Rev. Dominic Keller, who had me get up on the stage and give a prepared speech for my final. It scared the hell out of me! I have so many fond memories of my teachers at St. John's. I just wanted to share a few names with you in case you cross paths with any who are still there.

I shouldn't tell you boys this, but let's just say I didn't do too well at St. Thomas before I was admitted on "probation" to St. John's. I have Rev. Martin Schirber to thank for my turnaround. When he admitted me, he changed my life, and I'll be forever grateful to him.

That's enough of this reminiscing. If you ever meet any of my professors, please give them my best. Mom sends her love!

—Love, Dad

Michael: (Michael writes a letter to his parents and reads it out loud as he writes it so Mark can hear.)

October 9, 1970

Dear Mom and Dad,

Mark said he doesn't have any of the professors Dad described in his letter to us, nor do I. I'll say this, Dad, for going back eighteen years you sure remember a lot of them. One you didn't mention is Rev. Matthew Kiess, who was here during your time and is still teaching chemistry. He's a fixture in the chemistry lab and also heads the Chemistry Club, which I joined. Mark joined the Debate Club, which is obviously more in line with his pre-law courses. I'm going back over to St. Ben's with him next week for moral support, as his Debate Club will be debating the women of St. Ben's, and Mark's one of the debaters. Of course, I'm hoping to meet Laurie Johnson again while I'm there, and Mark the same with Linda Johnson.

That's all the news for now. It's back to studying for us.

—Love, Michael

Scene IV: The Debate

NARRATOR: Michael gets his wish of crossing paths with Laurie at the St. Ben's debate. She's right across the aisle from him in the auditorium. To Michael's amazement and unbeknownst to Mark, Linda Johnson is sitting up on the stage, directly across from his brother. She is going to be debating Mark! The audience grows silent as a neatly dressed middle-aged woman approaches the microphone near the front of the stage.

Sister Mary Elizabeth Collins: Good afternoon, ladies and gentlemen. My name is Sister Mary Elizabeth Collins, and I'm the Dean of Students at St. Benedict's College. I'd like to extend a special welcome to the debaters from St. John's University. All of us are in for an exciting program this afternoon.

As I'm sure you're all aware, earlier this year the United States Supreme Court began hearing a case concerning the rights of women to have abortions. This case began after a Texas waitress, who is referred to as "Jane Roe," challenged a Texas law that made abortion a criminal offense. Roe had been denied an abortion under the law and sued Dallas County District Attorney Henry Wade. With this topic presently being debated nationally by citizens of our country, it seemed only natural that we include it as one of our debate topics today. We'll begin with the affirmative speaker, Linda Johnson.

(Mark can barely conceal his shock at hearing the name of his debate opponent, none other than his new love! Linda rises calmly from her chair and walks confidently to the podium.)

Linda: Ladies and gentlemen, and my respected opponent, (Mark's face falls and Linda continues.) I stand before you today to prove that every woman should have the right to have an abortion in the United States. First, let us consider a woman's right to privacy. What could be more private to a woman than a fetus growing within her own body? Should the government be telling women what they can or cannot do with their own bodies? I should say not! Where will it end? Next, the government will be telling women what they can or cannot do in their bedrooms! Sounds crazy, but it could happen. It would be ridiculous and it would be wrong, just as is the thought of the government having control over choices a woman makes regarding her own body. That's a dictatorship, not a democracy!

(Mark's face grows grim. He listens intently and can't believe what he is hearing coming from the lips of the one with whom he is smitten!)

Linda: Have you ever researched women's rights in our country? Did you know that it wasn't until 1920 that the United States adopted the 19th amendment to the Constitution, granting American women the right to vote? Did you know that in the early 1900's the distribution of birth control information was illegal in the United States? Did you know that during World War II several million American women took factory production jobs to aid the war effort? When they were needed to win the war, they sure were given the right to do the work of men! But after the war, these same women were encouraged to become full-time housewives. Perhaps you're wondering what all this has to do with abortion. Well, it has everything to do with abortion because what women are asking for is the right to be treated as equals, not just when our country is threatened, but always!

(Linda takes a deep breath, pauses, and continues.)

Linda: In 1963, the Equal Pay Act came to be, which required equal pay for men and women doing the same work. In 1964, Title VII of the Civil Rights Act prohibited job discrimination on the basis of sex as well as well as color, race, national origin and religion. And now it's 1970, and are you telling me that the United States government should have the right to tell me what I should or shouldn't do with my body? Absolutely not!

(Linda pauses and looks out solemnly over the audience for several seconds before continuing.)

Linda: What all of this boils down to, ladies and gentlemen, is not simply the invasion of a woman's privacy or the curtailing of her rights as a citizen of this country; it's the removal of freedom, the freedom of a woman to choose when and if she should give birth to a child. If this freedom is taken from her, she is no longer living in the **"Land of the Free."**

(As Linda turns away from the podium and heads back to her seat, Sister Mary Elizabeth Collins rises and walks towards Mark to help guide him to the podium.)

Sister Mary Elizabeth Collins: Our next speaker is Mr. Mark Dowdle from St. John's University. Mark will be taking the negative position.

(Mark stands motionless at the podium for a few moments, nods acknowledgement in Linda's direction, and then turns to face the audience. After hearing Linda's eloquent presentation, he knows he's in for a fight, a real verbal battle, and he's ready to give it to her.)

Mark: (speaking slowly and seriously) Ladies and gentlemen, Miss Johnson has given us quite a history lesson today. I was happy to hear her closing remarks about choice, which is what I'd like to speak about this afternoon, freedom of choice, freedom to choose life or death for an unborn child.

As I listened to Miss Johnson attempting to make her case for abortion, I was thinking about the precious gift of life. I'd like to begin my remarks by reviewing for you the beginnings of that life and its early development. Once pregnancy begins, the embryo develops rapidly. Within two months, all the tissues and organs of the body have begun to form. The central nervous system, which consists of the brain and spinal cord, starts to develop in the third week of pregnancy. The eyes and ears begin to develop in the fourth week. The structures of the mouth, such as the lips and palate, begin to form between the fourth and fifth weeks of pregnancy. After that, the fetus increases rapidly in size until the mother gives birth to her child, the same child whose vibrant life Miss Johnson wishes to end.

(Mark could feel the rapt attention of the audience. One could have heard a pin drop. He waits, takes a deep breath, and continues.)

Mark: Does this mean there is never justification for terminating a pregnancy? No! In my opinion, there are exceptions, such as when a woman is traumatically impregnated due to rape or when the mother is in danger of losing her life due to medical complications. The Roman Catholic Church teaches that a doctor should attempt to save the lives of both the mother and the unborn child, but if this becomes impossible, I believe the mother's life should become the priority. During abortion discussions, the question of when life begins often arises. There's no question about that in my mind! A male delivers sperm to a female's egg, a remarkable moment of fertilization occurs, and thus begins the miraculous journey of human development!

(It is difficult for Mark to gauge the audience's reaction because of the tense silence in the room when he unexpectedly stops speaking. He turns towards Sister Mary Elizabeth, who rises quickly and guides him back to his seat before approaching the podium.)

Sister Mary Elizabeth: Those are the affirmative statements from each debater, ladies and gentlemen. Now we'll take a break of fifteen minutes before moving on to the rebuttals.

(After the break, the first speaker will be Linda. She sits in her seat with her head down and concentrates on her notes, flipping through pages and scribbling like crazy. Mark just sits quietly and seems to be gazing contentedly into space without concern. When the break ends, Sister Mary Elizabeth approaches the podium.)

Sister Mary Elizabeth: Thank you once again, ladies and gentlemen, for being with us this afternoon. I told you it would be an exciting program, and these two debaters did not disappoint us! It's now time for the rebuttals, and starting off will be Linda Johnson.

Linda: (turns and smiles at Mark) First I'd like to thank Mr. Dowdle for helping me make my point when he said he supports abortion in particular instances, believing it to be an appropriate procedure when a woman's life is at risk or she has been impregnated against her will. There are other times as well. I'd like to focus on just one of those since my opponent made such a great effort to give us a textbook version of when life begins and how it develops. Thank you, Mr. Dowdle, for the lesson, but unfortunately you failed to distinguish between human life and **personhood**. Personhood implies both the capacity for self-conscious thought and acceptance as a member of a social community. Can a fetus do that? Fetuses are not persons, and they're not entitled to the rights normally given to persons. Birth represents the beginning of personhood, Mr. Dowdle, and therefore abortion should be legal from conception until birth!

(With that, Linda turns and walks briskly to her seat. Mark waits for her to continue speaking, but hearing nothing, he realizes she is finished. She has ended her rebuttal in the same abrupt manner he ended his affirmative speech, and it takes him by surprise. Mark slowly rises from his chair as Sister Mary Elizabeth once again approaches him and leads him to the podium.)

Mark: Well, this is proving to be a very interesting afternoon.

(One can hear whispers and quiet chuckling ripple through the college audience as he continues.)

Mark: Miss Johnson began today by making a plea for a woman's privacy, rights, equality and freedom. I've prepared mentally to address each of those terms, but now she's introduced a new term, "personhood," so I'll begin with that. Miss Johnson stated that "personhood" implies both the capacity for self-conscious thought and acceptance as a member of a social community. She went on to say fetuses are not persons and are therefore not entitled to the rights normally given to persons. Birth represents the beginning of personhood according to my opponent, and therefore, she reasoned, abortion should be legal from conception until birth.

(Mark pauses, turns in Linda's direction, says nothing for a few seconds, and then continues.)

Mark: I hope I've accurately summed up your statements, Miss Johnson, because what you've said strikes me as being quite illogical. First of all, I don't believe you have the right to tell anyone who is and isn't a person! God took care of that when He created us! He created men and women and gave us the capacity to create other men and women. These other men and women didn't suddenly begin thinking as soon as they were born. It was a gradual process that began when a woman became impregnated and carried her child for nine months, then bore the child and began nurturing that child. In my opinion, it's an insult to "motherhood," Miss Johnson, to say that because a fetus hasn't been born that it doesn't qualify for personhood. The fact that a living, growing, developing fetus has the capacity for future life outside the womb is clearly enough to qualify for "personhood!"

(Mark pauses to let what he's just said sink in and then continues.)

Mark: Now let's move on to some of Miss Johnson's other arguments. First, let's consider her plea for privacy. I'll be the first to agree that what's happening in a woman's body during pregnancy is very private. She's experiencing a symbiotic relationship with a fetus that's growing inside her, and what business is that of the government? When these two beings, mother and fetus, have entered into a mutually beneficial relationship to produce life, then doesn't the government have the responsibility to help protect that life? Does not our constitution guarantee us the right to life, liberty, and the pursuit of happiness?

Notice, Miss Johnson, that I said "right to life" because I believe a fetus has rights, too. It's a living organism unable to speak for itself, thus the mother has the responsibility to speak on its behalf, and if she's unwilling, then the government has to step in and protect the rights of the unborn child. You folks will recall Miss Johnson speaking about the unfairness of women enduring far too many years of unequal rights compared to their male counterparts, and I certainly agree with that, but political, economic, and social rights don't fall into the same category as biological rights. If one isn't given the right to live, then every other right becomes irrelevant, not even debatable if one isn't given the right to exist and enjoy those other rights!

(Mark gazes out towards the hushed audience and pauses before making his closing statement.)

Mark: In closing, Miss Johnson, what I'm telling you is that it's every mother's right and responsibility to choose life, not death, for her unborn child, and that it's a magnificent gift of freedom that comes with being a privileged citizen of this country, and that we should all be filled with appreciation and gratitude on behalf of every miraculous life in the making!

(Mark turns towards where Sister Mary Elizabeth is sitting,

signaling that he is finished, but just as she rises, Linda, Mark's debate opponent, stands up quickly and approaches him at the podium. She puts her hand on his shoulder and then does something rarely seen at a debate. She leans her head near his cheek and kisses him! Mark's turns bright red, and he feels like his face is on fire as the audience begins hooting and whistling their approval.)

Mark: (grins from ear to ear and whispers to Linda) Was that a concession kiss I just felt on my cheek?

(Sister Mary Elizabeth approaches the podium and smiles at the debate contestants and then faces the audience.)

Sister Mary Elizabeth: Well, I told you this was going to be an exciting afternoon! In just a few minutes we'll have the judges' results, and then we'll proceed with the next debate.

(Linda links her arm with Mark's and exits with him from the stage.)

Linda: I hope you understand this was just a debate, Mark, and that I actually agree with your side. You did great!

Mark: Thanks, Linda. You were pretty impressive yourself.

(Linda and Mark find their seats, side by side in the audience, just as Sister Mary Elizabeth approaches the podium to announce the debate winner. The crowd hushes.)

Sister Mary Elizabeth: Ladies and gentlemen, our three judges have decided on a winner. Their decision is unanimous. They have decided that Miss Johnson has won this debate.

(Soft murmurings can be heard throughout the audience followed by a short applause.)

Sister Mary Elizabeth: I guess this means you'll have to continue this debate among yourselves. We'll now proceed to our next debate.

(It's close to dinnertime at the conclusion of the afternoon's final debate, and Sister Mary Elizabeth addresses the audience once again.)

Sister Mary Elizabeth: It certainly was a pleasure for all of us to hear these debaters in action! (Sister Mary Elizabeth pauses as the audience applauds and whistles loudly.) I hope we'll have an opportunity to do it again in the near future. This completes the debates for this afternoon, and I'd like to announce that the Saint John's University Debate Team and any other Johnnies in attendance are welcome to have dinner with us in the dining hall a half hour from now.

(Michael, who had been sitting with Laurie, approaches his brother alone and nudges him.)

Michael: Let's stay for dinner, Mark! Laurie told me the food is really good!

(Mark doesn't need any encouragement. His mind is still on the kiss Linda gave him on the cheek right after he finished his final remarks of the debate. Linda and Laurie have found one another, and they approach Mark and Michael.)

Linda: I hope you and Michael are staying for dinner, Mark.

Mark: Michael just told me the food is really good. You don't have to ask me twice. Let's go!

(As the foursome leave the auditorium and head towards the dining hall, Linda takes hold of Mark's hand to guide him.)

Linda: I hope I didn't embarrass you when I kissed you on the cheek. I was just so proud of you, and I had the urge to do it, so I did!

Mark: I'm glad you did! At first I thought it was Sister Mary Elizabeth Collins kissing me, and I wondered what the heck was going on! When I realized it was you, I knew everything was right with the world, debate or no debate!

Linda: You're so sweet!

Mark: And I realized another thing, too.

Linda: What's that?

Mark: That there is such a thing as love at first sight! (Mark smiles, squeezes Linda's hand, and whispers) I think I'm falling in love with you, Linda Johnson!

Scene V: Dinner at St. Ben's

(Linda squeezes Mark's hand, but says nothing as they enter the dining hall. The tables are covered with white tablecloths and have place settings with shiny silverware and cloth napkins. Michael describes the scene to his brother.)

Michael: This feels like a ritzy restaurant! You girls are treated like queens here!

Laurie: (laughing) Of course!

(After they're seated, Sister Mary Elizabeth and several other "Bennie" coeds join Linda, Laurie, Mark and Michael at their table. Everyone grows silent as Sister Mary Elizabeth stands and tinkles her glass with her knife and begins to pray.)

Sister Mary Elizabeth: *Dear Lord, thank you for blessing us with the many gifts we've been able to enjoy today and for the beautiful meal we now have the privilege of sharing with the visiting students from St. John's. Amen.*

(A bevy of Bennies carrying large, white porcelain bowls brimming with steaming mashed potatoes and green beans comes briskly walking from the kitchen. They're followed by other Bennies carrying platters piled high with layers of sliced roast beef.)

Sister Mary Elizabeth: (jovially) Let the feast begin! I sure hope you boys like roast beef.

Mark: So happens it's one of our favorite meals! We used to have it quite often at home on Sundays. Our dad loves it, and our mom is an exceptional cook!

Sister Mary Elizabeth: Well, we probably can't compete with your mom's home-cooked version, but I'm glad it's a meal you'll enjoy. I'll stop talking now and let you young people eat and visit.

(A Bennie freshman sitting across from Linda smiles at her and asks her a question.)

Bennie freshman: Did you and Laurie know Michael and Mark before you came to St. Ben's? I noticed you leaving the debate together and you seem like longtime close friends.

Linda: (laughing) Well, longtime, no, but we did meet these two at the dance we hosted for the Johnnies in September.

Mark: (enthusiastically) And we were happy to meet them!

Michael: (laughing) I'll ditto that!

(After everyone is finished eating the main meal and the empty dishes are removed, the Bennie servers again emerge from the kitchen, this time pushing rolling carts with dessert plates filled with generous slices of cherry pie topped with hefty scoops of vanilla ice cream.)

Michael: (nudges Mark) Cherry pie and vanilla ice cream for dessert!

Mark: Did I somehow arrive in heaven? (Everyone laughs.)

(When it comes time to leave, Mark and Linda and Michael and Laurie are standing outside waiting for a Johnnie bus to arrive. It has grown dark, and the cool October air breezes against their faces.)

Mark: (draws Linda close to his side and whispers) I'd like to return that kiss you gave me after the debate. I have the urge, just like you said you had!

(Mark smiles as Linda draws her face close to his and their warm lips press softly together. Then a contagion sets in. Michael and Laurie embrace, they look into each other's eyes, and Laurie closes hers as Michael gently kisses her.)

Michael: (laughs as he sees the Johnnie bus coming around the corner) Darn, there's the bus!

(Everyone says their goodbyes and the bus is soon heading back to St. John's.)

Fellow Johnnie: (sitting across the aisle from Mark and Michael) How long have you two known those gals? A bunch of us couldn't help notice what good friends you are.

Michael: We met at the September mixer at St. Ben's.

Fellow Johnnie: (laughing) Good for you! You two are a couple of fast workers!

Michael: (smiling) Double fast!

(During the ride back to the university, everyone seems content to just sit quietly and think about the debates and the hearty meal they've just eaten. The bus arrives at St. John's and Michael and Mark are walking towards St. Mary's hall.)

Michael: Well, Mark, what do you think?

Mark: (answers slowly) I think…I'm in love!

Michael: (playfully nudges his brother) Are you kidding?

Mark: Not at all! I think Linda is the girl for me!

Michael: Funny thing is, I feel the same way about Laurie!

ACT III:
LOVE AND MARRIAGE

Scene I: The Pre-Christmas Dance

NARRATOR: The twins are kept busy with their studies during the rest of October and November, as are Linda and Laurie. When December arrives, Michael and Mark learn that St. John's will be hosting an all-class pre-Christmas dance before Christmas vacation, and they grow very excited.

Mark: We should invite Linda and Laurie to the Johnnie Christmas dance, Michael! It's a by-invitation-only event! Perfect opportunity to get together with them before we head home for Christmas!

Michael: (voice filled with excited anticipation) Couldn't be better timing, Brother! If it's all right with you, I'll call Laurie and ask if Linda and she will do us the honor of being our dates!

Mark: (very excitedly) Please do! I can hardly wait!

(A light snow is falling the night of the dance, bright stars are twinkling against an ebony sky, and a full moon is lighting the way as Michael and Mark leave St. Benedict's with the girls and drive the short distance on the freeway and onto the snow-packed road through the woods to St. John's.)

Laurie: This is beautiful!

Linda: I'm so excited, Mark! This will be the first time I've seen your campus!

Mark: I never have!

(Mark smiles and everyone breaks out in laughter at his self-deprecating sense of humor.)

Mark: I think you're going to like being here. Michael and I sure do!

(The dance is held in the gym, which is cozily lit and festively decorated for Christmas. A large tableau of the Holy Family fills one corner and aromatic evergreens laced with golden lights are positioned strategically among tables lining the edges of the gym floor.)

Linda: I love this, Mark! (reaches for his hand) I love the smell of the pine trees!

(All Mark hears is the word "love" among the words Linda has just spoken, and that's all the encouragement he needs. The two couples barely find a table when the band begins playing "White Christmas," a holiday favorite.)

Michael: Aha! A nice slow number!

Mark: Would you ladies like to dance?

Linda and Laurie: (answering in unison) Of course!

(The two couples wend their way to the dance floor and begin moving slowly and melting into each others' arms, Linda resting her head on Mark's shoulder as he holds her close, Michael and Laurie gazing into each others' eyes.)

Laurie: Thank you for inviting us to the dance, Michael. This is far more thrilling than studying!

Michael: I hope so! Mark and I jumped at the chance to invite you two. You can probably tell we're smitten!

(Laurie can feel herself blushing and beginning to feel warm all over and is grateful for the darkened gym. Michael can feel the effect of his words on her as the band plays on and she melts warmly into his arms.)

NARRATOR: On the drive back to St. Ben's, Michael and Mark both sense that Laurie and Linda are very happy with the way the evening unfolded. When they reach St. Ben's, the brothers walk the girls to their dormitory, embrace them, kiss them goodnight and head back to St. John's.

Michael: Brother, we're in trouble!

Mark: I'll say! Double trouble!

NARRATOR: When they get home for Christmas vacation, Mark and Michael are kept busy shopping for presents and visiting with their friends, and the two weeks seem to fly by. Before you know it, Christmas vacation is over, and the boys are ready to hop in the station wagon and go back to school.

Mark: (hesitantly) Dad, Mom, before Michael and I head back to St. John's, we have to tell you something important.

Marty: (worriedly) What's that Mark?

Mark: I think something very serious has happened to Michael and me!

Marty: What happened, Mark?

Mark: Michael and I have fallen madly in love with the Johnson twins!

Michael: Mark is telling the truth, Mom. We have!

Chuck: (laughing at his sons) Well, boys, it won't be the first time a fellow has fallen hard for a beautiful female. Just look at your mom and me!

Marty: Just do your best at school, boys, and we'll talk about your love lives when you come home for summer vacation.

Scene II: Summer Vacation

NARRATOR: Mark and Michael buckle down for their first semester finals when they return to St. John's after Christmas vacation, and it pays off. They both receive straight A's in all of their classes and they are two proud Johnnies. The second semester is a little different. Time seems to move more slowly, and when the snow melts in April and pink blossoms appear on the trees in May, both boys experience spring fever like never before, not to mention the fact that their male hormones are running rampant. So, you can imagine the twins' exuberance when they get home for summer vacation and Linda calls.

Linda: Hi, Mark! This is Linda! Laurie and I were wondering if Michael and you would be interested in visiting us at our parents' house sometime this summer with your parents?

Mark: We'd love to!

Linda: Okay! I'll arrange a time with my parents and get back to you. It'll be great seeing you and Michael again, Mark.

Mark: I feel the same Linda. I can hardly wait!

(Mark mentions Linda's call to his brother.)

Mark: Guess what, Michael? We've been invited to the Johnsons to visit Linda and Laurie this summer. Do you want to go? (smiles)

Michael: Are you kidding? You don't have to ask me twice! It'll be great!

NARRATOR: What the boys don't know is that they're going to be put to work now that they're home, and that the work is going to last the entire summer. While they've been away at college, Marty has started working full time at St. James Hospital and Chuck has begun selling *World Book Encyclopedia* to libraries, schools and parents in a wider geographical area than he had in the past. He's now selling in small towns around Perham and even some of the larger ones like Detroit Lakes, Fergus Falls and Wadena.

The summer proves to be quite a learning experience for Mark and Michael. They drive with their dad to one of the small towns such as New York Mills and begin knocking on doors, handing out cards, and giving *World Book* sales demonstrations. At first Chuck does pretty much all of the talking, and gradually the twins add to his spiel by explaining just how useful *World Book* had been for them throughout their lives. Mark brings the braille "A" volume along and clinches many a sale as he wows prospective buyers with his advanced reading skills. Before long the boys are knocking on doors by themselves and surprising Chuck with their impressive sales.

While celebrating their eighteenth birthday with their parents on August 9, 1971, the boys break the news to them about being invited to visit the Johnsons before school starts.

Mark: Mom, Dad, we've got something to ask you.

Marty: What is it, Mark?

Mark: Michael and I have been invited to visit the Johnsons in Coon Rapids at the end of the month before school starts, and we were wondering if that would be all right with you?

Marty: (smiles at her two beaming sons) This must be getting very serious!

Mark: It is, Mom! Linda is a lot like you. She's bright and loving, soft-spoken and so compassionate. I just can't get enough of her!

Michael: And I can't stop thinking about Laurie! She's a beautiful person through and through! I love that girl!

Chuck: Well, how would you feel if your mother and I drove down with you?

Mark: We'd love it! You've been invited, too!

Marty: Wow! This *is* getting serious!

Chuck: Tell me! It'll be fun meeting your future in-laws!

> (Chuck's remark brings smiles and laughs to all of the birthday celebrants.)

Marty: Well, I think it's time to cut the cake and get on with your birthday celebration, boys! This has all been a little too exciting for me!

NARRATOR: The next couple of weeks roll by quickly and it is soon the end of August, time for Marty, Chuck and their sons to head to Coon Rapids to visit the Johnsons. The twins are gushing with anticipation, as they haven't seen their girlfriends all summer. That is only part of the excitement, however. At ten o'clock on Saturday morning, the day before they're leaving, Chuck's friend from St. John's, Perham automobile dealer Tom Schmitz, drives up in a brand-new, four-door silver sedan. He parks in front of the house and just sits there.

Michael: (glancing curiously out the kitchen window) That's Tom Schmitz sitting out there in a new car, Dad. Looks like he came to show you some fancy new wheels!

Chuck: Why don't you run out and ask him what's up. I'll be right there.

(As Michael walks towards the shiny new 1971 Ford, Tom gets out and dangles the keys in his hand.)

Tom: How do you like her, Michael?

Michael: That's one good-looking car, Tom! Is it yours?

Tom: (smiling) No, Michael. It's a recent purchase by your mom and dad.

Michael: (laughing) You're kidding! Why would they do that when they already have a new car?

Tom: (grinning from ear to ear) Because this baby belongs to you and Mark! Your folks bought it for the two of you because the station wagon's so old.

(Michael can't believe his ears. He turns and runs towards the house just as Marty, Chuck and Mark open the front door and step onto the porch.)

Chuck: Well, what do you think, Michael?

Michael: (yells) I can't believe it! Mark, it's ours! A brand-new, four-door silver Ford sedan!

Mark: (stunned) What? Dad, Mom, why?

Michael: (shouting) Questions later, Mark! C'mon, check it out!

(Michael takes his brother's hand and they both rush down the walk toward their new car. When they reach it, Mark moves his hands slowly along the smooth, warm metallic side before feeling for the handle and opening the front passenger door.)

Mark: (guides himself onto the front passenger seat) It smells wonderfully new!

(Michael runs around to the driver's side and jumps in next to his brother.)

Mark: (asking with incredulity as he runs his hands along the smooth dashboard) Is this for real?

Michael: (gleefully) I guess so! I still can't believe it!

Mark: (shakes his head in disbelief) This is so generous of Mom and Dad! (pauses) I wonder if they'll let us drive it to Coon Rapids tomorrow?

Michael: (gets out of car and walks toward the house with Mark) Let's go find out!

(Marty and Chuck are standing on the front porch, chatting with Tom Schmitz.)

Marty: How do you boys like your new car?

Mark and Michael: (in unison as they hug their parents) We love it! Thank you! Thank you! Thank you!

Michael: It sure will make for a sweet drive to St. John's compared to the old wagon!

Mark: (smiling) And Linda and Laurie will think we're really hot stuff!

Michael: Speaking of impressing our girlfriends, do you think we could drive it to Coon Rapids tomorrow when we go to the Johnsons?

Chuck: Of course! That's the reason we wanted it delivered today. We'll hit the road right after Sunday Mass.

(They say goodbye to Tom and can't stop talking about gliding along Highway 78 in their shiny new silver sedan to the Johnsons' house the next morning.)

Michael: This is going to be so much fun! I can't believe it!

Mark: You're going to be the driver, Michael. You'd better take it easy! That baby will jump out a lot faster than the old wagon.

Michael: You worry too much! Just leave the driving to me!

NARRATOR: Sunday morning arrives, and the Dowdle-Johnson introductions are soon to be. As is customary when they travel, the Dowdle family says the rosary together as they roll along in the new Ford. They approach Coon Rapids, and Michael pulls up in front of the Johnsons' beautiful church, the Church of the Epiphany.

Michael: I thought you might like to stop and see where the Johnsons go to church.

Chuck: We certainly have the time, Michael, and it would be an excellent place to pray that all goes well with our visit!

(After kneeling and saying a few silent, personal prayers, Marty describes the inside of the church to Mark on their way out. She also picks up a parish bulletin and reads it to herself on the way to the car.)

Marty: Listen to this. It's the mission statement of the Church of the Epiphany from the parish bulletin. I'll read it to you while we're driving to the Johnsons' house:

"We the people of Epiphany Parish have built a growing community on Coon Rapids farmland since our beginning in 1964. We are a parish with educational priorities. We are a caring people who minister by reaching out to our brothers and sisters, responding to their physical and spiritual needs. We will manifest Christ through fostering spiritual growth and unity, and witnessing our faith."

"Lighting the Way to Christ"

Mark: Wow! That's a pretty impressive statement. Thanks for reading it to us, Mom.

Michael: We're just about there, folks. Perfect timing! Two o'clock, right on schedule!

(Michael guides the sedan slowly and smoothly alongside the curb in front of the Johnsons' house. Anticipating their arrival, Linda is looking out the window, and when she sees Mark and Michael arrive with their parents, she runs out of the house and down the walk to greet them, almost knocking Mark over with a hearty embrace as he steps from the car.

Mark is taken by surprise, and so is everyone else. Laurie soon comes running out of the house as well, and when she sees Michael, it's another hug fest! Mr. Johnson walks towards the car to greet Chuck and Marty.)

Mr. Johnson: (laughing as he shakes hands with Chuck) Walter Johnson, Chuck. A pleasure. It seems my daughters are pretty overjoyed to see your sons!

Chuck: (smiling) So I see, Walter, and I'm sure you noticed my sons beaming from ear to ear!

Mrs. Johnson: (calling enthusiastically from the front porch) C'mon in, everybody! Let's all head to the living room for some formal introductions and get to know each other! It's going to be a little while before we eat.

(Everyone enters the house and settles comfortably in the cozy living room. The boys make their introductions with such enthusiastic fanfare that the parents can't help but applaud and cheer them on in honor of young love.)

Mark: I don't know how Michael and I got so lucky. I haven't been able to stop thinking about Linda ever since I first met her.

(Linda reaches for Mark's hand, squeezes it in hers, turns warm all over and blushes. Michael smiles as he puts his hands in Laurie's and pulls her close to him.)

Michael: Lucky is right! Mark and I still can't believe it! We feel blessed and loved!

(After all the introductions and some relaxed time to just talk casually, the Johnsons take everyone on a grand tour of the house. First up are all the bathrooms, a necessity with four guests. Many wows and words of wonder can be heard coming from Marty and Chuck as they admire the spacious, airy kitchen and elegant master bedroom.)

Marty: This bedroom suite is as large as the whole first floor of our house!

Walter: Well, Marty, it's roomy, no doubt about that, but I'm a home builder, and I've built a lot of homes, and if there's one thing Grace and I like in a house, it's lots of space!

Chuck: You've sure got that here, Walter!

(Chuck and Marty and the boys bring their suitcases to their guest rooms, unpack and are washing up when an old fashioned dinner bell is heard ringing from the kitchen.)

Grace: (calling loudly) Time to eat! Everyone come to the dining room!

(A very large rectangular table capable of seating sixteen is elegantly set for eight in the middle of the room.)

Chuck: (smiling before he sits) This feels a little like the Last Supper!

(Everyone laughs and sits: Chuck opposite Walter, Marty opposite Grace, Mark opposite Linda, and Michael opposite Laurie. There isn't any question about where to sit. Linda and Laurie have printed first names on cards to go with each place setting.)

Walter: This is a very special occasion, and we've got a lot to be thankful for. Let's pray: *Lord, we thank you for this wonderful meal we're about to be served and for letting us all be together to celebrate the end of summer and the start of a new school year for our children and the beginning of new and lasting friendships.*

Grace: *And loves!*

Everyone: *Amen!*

(Immediately, as if they'd been given a cue in a play, Linda and Laurie hop up from their chairs and head for the kitchen.)

Laurie: Everyone stay seated, Linda and I have got this!

(Linda is the first to emerge with a large ivory platter filled with steaming golden-brown sliced turkey.)

Mark: (inhaling deeply) Something smells like Thanksgiving!

(Laurie emerges from the kitchen with another large ivory platter piled high with thick juicy slices of ham.)

Michael: And I see ham, too, Mark!

Grace: (laughing) With the eight of us, we thought we'd better have both. We don't want anyone going away hungry!

(Linda and Laurie continue carrying out an array of side dishes and placing them on the table.)

Chuck: By the looks of all this food, I don't think you're going to have to worry about that Grace!

Marty: It all looks so wholesome and appetizing!

Michael: (looking at Grace) Laurie and Linda must have told you how much Mark and I enjoy eating.

Grace: (proudly) I'll have you know the girls fixed this entire meal by themselves! They wouldn't let me do a thing!

Walter: (laughing) I think they wanted to impress you boys.

Mark: (smiling) Consider it done! I'm impressed!

Michael: No question about that!

(Their boyfriends' comments bring a big smile to the girls' faces.)

Linda: And we made a pumpkin pie and an apple pie for dessert, so leave room!

(Everyone feasts on the turkey and ham dinner. Linda and Laurie clear away the dishes and emerge from the kitchen, this time carrying two beautiful pies and a large bowl of whipped cream.)

Michael: (eyeing the pies as they make their way around the table) Two pies, Mark! I think I'm going to have to try a piece of each! They both look wonderful!

Mark: (savoring his first bite of pumpkin pie) You girls outdid yourselves! This pie is delicious!

(Everyone finishes dessert and Linda and Laurie once again clear away all the dishes.)

Grace: Let's all move into the living room where we can get comfortable and talk.

Marty: Good idea, Grace, and I want to thank you right now for including Chuck and me with your invitation to our sons. Everything was delightful!

Grace: Marty, it was our pleasure, and I think we're going to be seeing a lot more of each other. C'mon, let's go into the living room and talk.

(After a good night's sleep and a hearty breakfast the next morning, the Dowdle family packs up and is ready to drive back to Perham.)

Marty: Thank you once again for including us in your invitation. It was wonderful being able to meet all of you. And I can see why my sons are in love with your daughters.

(After several rounds of hugs, goodbyes and kisses, the Dowdles are soon on the road and heading back to Perham.)

Marty: You boys certainly have a couple of sweet girlfriends, and I sure enjoyed meeting Walter and Grace.

Chuck: I feel the same as your mom. The twins are great gals and Walter and Grace are going to make some really neat in-laws!

Marty: (laughing) I think you're rushing things a little, Chuck.

Mark: (coyly) Maybe not! Maybe not!

(The boys' parents exchange smiling glances and settle into the comfortable back seat of the new Ford sedan for a quiet and restful ride back to Perham.)

Michael: (whispering softly to Mark as they pull into the driveway) We're here, Mark.

(Marty and Chuck have dozed off, and it is little wonder. They'd eaten a sumptuous dinner the night before with their new acquaintances, a big breakfast in the morning, they're nestled in a warm and comfortable new car, and they're tired!)

NARRATOR: The next morning everyone is up early and ready and raring to go, Marty to St. James Hospital, Chuck to Perham High School to prep for a new school year, and the boys packing for their drive back to St. John's. Before she leaves, Marty gives each of her sons a big hug.

Marty: Now you be careful driving that new car, Michael! Not too fast!

Mark: (joking) Don't worry, Mom. I'll keep an eye on him.

NARRATOR: Both boys have heard their mom's admonitions many times before, and they know it's just her way of telling them how much she loves them. They love their mother, as well, of course, but the love they have for her is different from their love for Linda and Laurie. That's a man to woman love, a passionate love, and they can hardly wait to get back to school to take advantage of the first opportunity to see Linda and Laurie again.

When they aren't occupied with their studies, Mark and Michael drive to St. Ben's on the weekends to see Linda and Laurie, and their relationships develop and deepen over the next two years. During their daughters' senior year, the Johnsons once again invite Chuck and Marty and their sons to their Coon Rapids home for Christmas Eve dinner and a Christmas day celebration. A lot has happened in the two years since they last saw them in the summer of 1971, and they have a lot of catching up to do. Grace has a feeling that something important is about to take place.

Scene III: The Proposal

NARRATOR: With an abundance of snow on the ground, it isn't an easy drive to Coon Rapids, but it doesn't seem to bother Mark or Michael. Their minds are elsewhere. Something is definitely happening between the twins, something about which Marty and Chuck don't have a clue, but they can certainly sense mystery in the air. When they pull up in front of the Johnson house, they're greeted by a magical scene, pine trees sparkling with holiday lights and a large tableau of Joseph, Mary, and the baby Jesus in a stable, complete with three wise men and an array of farm animals gathered around. It is lovely to behold and a reminder of the true meaning of Christmas.

(Linda is looking out the picture window at the Christmas scene when she sees the silver Ford sedan pull up in front of the house. She dashes out, and the moment Mark steps from the car, she wraps her arms around him.)

Linda: I'm so happy to see you!

(The two of them stand there in a tight embrace, oblivious to the snow on the ground and the chill in the air. Next up is Laurie, who rushes from the house and repeats the enthusiastic greeting with Michael. Finally, Chuck and Marty get out of the car just as Grace and Walter appear on the front porch. As Chuck and Marty slip and slide their way up the front walk, their children are still in a tight embrace. Walter steps from the porch and greets Chuck with a warm handshake as Grace and Marty embrace.)

Walter: Hi, Chuck and Marty! I'm so glad you could make it.

Marty: We're delighted to be here! Thank you for having us!

Walter: Those kids of ours are really in love!

Chuck: Tell me about it! Your daughters were the topic of conversation all the way here, Walter.

Walter: Well, your boys couldn't have fallen for two nicer girls than Linda and Laurie!

(Grace and Marty walk into the house behind the men.)

Grace: I heard that Walter, and I may be a little biased in favor of my daughters, but I wholeheartedly agree with you, and vice versa I might add, about Marty and Chuck's sons!

(They all remove their winter coats in the entryway, and Linda and Laurie, who have entered the house with their men after separating from their long embraces, take the coats down the hall to hang them up in a large walk-in closet.)

Mark: (inhaling deeply) The house smells like evergreens! I love it!

Linda: (gently linking her arm through Mark's) Let's go into the living room, Mark. The Christmas tree is in there.

(Everyone soon follows and settles comfortably in front of a blazing fire.)

Marty: Everything looks so beautiful in here! The tree is lovely!

Mark: I love the sound of the crackling fire! I can feel the heat!

Grace: We won't be eating for a little while, so why don't we just catch up on what's been happening with everyone since you were last here.

Chuck: Go ahead, Marty. You can get us started.

Marty: Well, let's see. The boys had finished their freshman year at St. John's in 1971 when we were here visiting that summer, and I began working as a physical therapist at St. James Hospital in Perham. I'm still doing that and enjoying every day of it. The boys come home from college during the holidays and summer vacation, and it's a full time job just keeping them fed, as you know all too well from their time here.

(Everyone laughs.)

Marty: Other than that, I've been getting in some reading and some long walks and fun bike rides with Chuck in the neighborhood and around town.

Chuck: It's been real busy for me. There's never a dull moment with teaching, and now that I'm Chair of the English Department, I organize the curriculum and evaluate the staff. It all takes time, but it seems the bulk of my time during the school year is spent grading papers. The boys and I have been busy during the summers selling *World Book Encyclopedia* around Otter Tail County, and that's been a big help financially, especially with the expense of two kids in college. Michael and Mark have become exceptional encyclopedia salesmen!

Michael: No complaints here. It's been fun! Mark and I have learned how to sell books, and when we add the money we've earned doing that to our scholarships, we feel extremely fortunate.

(All eyes are on Michael as he pauses for a moment and smiles at Laurie before continuing.)

Michael: (facing Grace and Walter) I know I speak for Mark, as well, when I tell you that the best thing that's ever happened to Mark and me has been falling in love with your beautiful daughters!

Mark: I couldn't have said it any better, Brother. (Mark rises slowly and gently pulls Linda to her feet.) However, I would like to add a little something.

(All eyes are on Mark. He and Michael planned this moment many months ago, and the time has finally come! Mark slowly kneels down in front of Linda and looks up at her. He reaches out for her hands, and she, sensing what is about to happen, willingly places hers in his. Then Mark speaks to her very softly, seriously, and reverently.)

Mark: Linda Johnson, you are a beautiful person in every way and I love you with all my heart. I can't imagine not spending every day of the rest of my life with you. Will you do me the honor of becoming my wife?

(The parents gasp with surprise, except for a beaming Walter. Mark and Michael had secretly sought his approval several weeks before. A flood of tears comes streaming down Linda's cheeks as she looks into Mark's eyes.)

Mark: (nervously) I don't know how long I'm supposed to wait to hopefully hear a yes!

(Everyone laughs.)

Linda: (ecstatically) Yes! Mark! Yes! You know I will!

(Mark reaches into his coat pocket, takes out a sparkling diamond ring, smiles up at Linda and slowly places the ring on her outstretched finger.)

Linda: Oh, Mark! It's beautiful! I love you so much!

(The parents applaud and Michael and Laurie cheer. Laurie then stands and embraces her sister, and Mark stands and shakes hands with his brother.)

Michael: Congratulations, Brother!

(Love is in the air! There are hugs all around! Laurie herself has barely recovered from all of her sister's excitement when she settles back onto the sofa next to Michael, who immediately stands, pulls her gently to her feet and kneels down in front of her! Their eyes meet, and Michael's so excited he feels like his heart might burst from his chest! The room becomes very quiet.)

Michael: Laurie Johnson, I've been in love with you from the moment we met, and every day that love has grown stronger! Will you make me the happiest man on this earth and marry me?

Laurie: (answers enthusiastically without hesitation) Yes, Michael! I will! I will! I love you!

(Another round of clapping and cheering ensues as Michael slips a sparkling diamond ring onto Laurie's outstretched finger. Her eyes well up with tears.)

Laurie: Oh, Michael, it's so beautiful!

Michael: (yelling) She said YES! She said YES!

(Everyone laughs. The two sets of newly-engaged couples embrace and kiss, Walter and Chuck shake hands, Grace and Marty exchange heartfelt hugs, and everyone carries on in joyful fashion, boisterous in their approval of the afternoon's happenings.)

Grace: (gleefully) Well, this certainly was a pleasant surprise! You boys did a good job of keeping it secret! (winks and smiles at her future sons-in-law) You, too, Walter! I bet you had this planned for a long time!

Walter: Too long!

Grace: Well, let's get ready to eat! I don't know how much more excitement I can take on an empty stomach!

(Everyone laughs and heads towards the dining room. Instead of sitting down, Marty follows Grace and the girls into the kitchen. Grace holds out her arms towards Marty and the two women embrace as tears of joy stream down their faces. Laurie and Linda join them, and the scene turns into a mother-daughter cry-fest. A few minutes elapse and Walter calls out jokingly.)

Walter: What's going on? We're starving out here!

NARRATOR: The large rectangular table is set lavishly for eight people, with an Advent wreath centerpiece formed with wire and freshly cut evergreens. Four colorful candles, three purple and one pink, are nestled in the evergreens equidistant from one another. A large white candle graces the center of the ring. All five candles are lit. The four smaller candles symbolize faith, hope, joy and love, and the large white candle, which is lit on Christmas Eve, is known as Christ's candle.

Walter: (turns towards Mark and Michael and smiles) I knew it was going to happen sometime today, I just didn't know when! Good job, boys!

Chuck: And I knew you two were a little antsy about something on the drive down here, but you certainly surprised us, and you chose the perfect time to do it. I don't know how you kept it a secret.

(The kitchen door swings open and Grace and Marty, each toting a bottle of fine white wine, enter first. Linda and Laurie enter next with two large platters of sliced ham. The procession continues as Grace and Marty return from the kitchen again with steaming bowls of candied yams and scalloped potatoes. Then Linda and Laurie arrive with peas and carrots and a festive salad. The enticing aroma of the food fills the air. The Advent wreath is glowing and emitting a soft, warm light as the ladies take their seats.)

Walter: Well, it looks like we're ready. Let's all hold hands and I'll say a prayer: *Lord, thank you for these kids of ours, as they sure are something special. They could not have made us any happier than we are at this moment. We love them and hope their futures together will be filled with joy, joy such as Chuck and I have found with our beautiful wives. We thank you for blessing us with our children and for this bountiful food that is spread before us. Amen.*

Everyone: (in unison) *Amen!*

Walter: I'd like to propose a toast! To Linda and Mark, Laurie and Michael, may your futures together shine as brightly as the light from Christ's candle as you prepare for your lives together.

(Everyone clinks their glasses, sips their wine, and appreciates the toast given in celebration of partnerships filled with faith, hope and love! Michael's eyes grow wide as the platters of food make their way around the table, juicy sliced ham, golden-brown scalloped potatoes, peas and carrots bursting with color. It is indeed a Christmas feast!)

Grace: (yelling, as she gets up and runs to the kitchen) I'll be back in a flash! I forgot the rolls!

(Grace returns with a basket of golden-brown dinner rolls piled high with fresh creamery butter on the side.)

Michael: Mrs. Johnson, you sure know how to cook! This meal is spectacular!

Mark: Sure is!

Grace: Well, I'm glad you two like my cooking! You'll hopefully be here often to enjoy a whole lot more of it!

NARRATOR: After dinner, which includes apple pie and vanilla ice cream for dessert, everyone is content and ready to plop down in the living room by the cozy fire. There isn't much talk before Walter and Chuck's heads drop downward and they're snoring up a storm. Grace and Marty just shake their heads, smile, gently wake their husbands and head off to bed with everyone else.

After exchanging gifts and enjoying a delicious Christmas breakfast the next morning, everyone piles into their cars and drives to the Church of the Epiphany for Mass. The beautifully decorated church is packed, so it's good they left the house early. During Holy Communion, it takes a long, long time because everyone receives. As they're leaving the church after Mass, Marty and Grace walk together towards their cars.

Marty: Thank you so much for having us. Chuck and I have enjoyed this time with you and Walter and the girls immensely, Grace, and it's certainly turned out to be a memorable Christmas!

Grace: Marty, I think your sons did it right. We already loved them like they were our own sons, and now they'll be a permanent part of the family! I'm so happy!

Marty: I feel the same about your daughters, Grace. We're going to have a lot of talking to do once they decide when and where they're getting married. I'm guessing it'll be a double-ring ceremony, but who knows! Whatever it is, whenever it is, I'll be looking forward to helping out however I can!

NARRATOR: Marty doesn't have to wait long for her answer. On the drive back to Perham, getting married is all the boys want to talk about. They're definitely anticipating a two-for-one affair, and they think it would be a good idea to plan for the wedding as soon as possible after graduation so they can have some honeymoon time during the summer before they start graduate school at the University of Minnesota. Now all they have to do is discuss it with their brides-to-be. When they do, Linda and Laurie more than agree.)

Linda: (enthusiastically) The sooner the better as far as we're concerned! Graduation is June 22nd at St. Benedict's.

Michael: June 3rd at St. John's.

Laurie: We could get married that next week on the 9th if that would work out with our folks.

Mark: I think it would be a perfect time. Dad will be out of school, and Mom and he usually like to go someplace and do something fun after working all year.

Laurie: Your mom and dad can stay at our house the week before the wedding if they want to, Michael. That would make it easy for our moms to be together for all the last-minute preparations. I'm sure they'd like that.

NARRATOR: Well, that's what happens. Mark and Michael graduate with honors, and on June 5th, four days before the wedding, the Dowdle family heads to Coon Rapids, but not before a bit of excitement at home!

After the St. John's graduation ceremony on June 3rd, Chuck and Marty drive back home to Perham to take care of a few things before packing up and heading to Coon Rapids for their week with the Johnsons. Part of that includes having Tom Schmitz deliver a new 1975 silver, four-door Ford sedan, just like the one they had purchased for themselves the year before!

When Michael and Mark pull up to the house the next day and Michael sees two identical silver sedans sitting at the curb, he tells Mark and they both wonder what's happening. Certainly their mom and dad wouldn't be trading in their new car already! Granted, Tom Schmitz is quite a salesman, but this wouldn't be like their parents. They usually keep their cars until they register at least 100,000 miles or more on the odometer.

Michael: Hey, Dad, what's going on with the new car out front?

Chuck: Well, that's something your mom and I will talk over with Mark and you after supper.

(Marty was unable to contain her excitement and was the first to speak up as they were finishing eating.)

Marty: That new car sitting by the curb outside belongs to your dad and me, boys! We just bought it from Tom Schmitz!

Mark: Wow! You two just bought a new car last year! Now you'll each have one!

Marty: (smiling excitedly) No we won't! You and Michael will!

Michael (incredulously) Us?

Chuck: That's right! We talked it over and decided that the car you're already driving and the one we bought for ourselves last year would make a couple of nice wedding presents for you and your new wives. We're giving them to you and keeping the new one that's sitting out front. How does that sound?

Michael: (flabbergasted) I can't believe it! Thank you! (gets up and hugs his parents) This is really going to help us! It's almost too much to handle!

Mark: (laughing) I think I'll handle it just fine once it sinks in! Thank you, Mom and Dad! (gets up and hugs his parents)

Marty: You boys deserve it! And Linda and Laurie, too! Tomorrow we'll drive all three cars to Coon Rapids.

Mark: Boy, is Linda ever going to be surprised! We've been talking about how we'll handle transportation to the university. Now that problem is solved thanks to you. You have no idea how much this gift is appreciated. We can't thank you enough!

Chuck: Well, Mark, you and Michael have absolutely earned it. I'm so proud of both of you and so happy that you'll soon be marrying two wonderful women. When we get to Coon Rapids tomorrow morning, you can walk with Linda out to the front of the house and give her the keys to your new car.

Marty: Right now we should be thinking about finishing our packing and getting to bed before it gets to be too late.

NARRATOR: The three silver sedans leave Perham bright and early the next morning and arrive in Coon Rapids just before noon. Linda is the first one out of the house to greet them, and she does a triple take when she sees the trio of matching cars. Mark steps out as she opens the front passenger door, and before anything else happens or is said, the two of them stand in a long embrace. Laurie runs down the walkway to greet Michael and he greets her with open arms and lifts her off her feet, swinging her around in a tight, happy embrace.

Walter: (calls to his daughters) Okay, you two. Let's remember Mark and Michael's parents are our honored guests as well!

Grace: And your future in-laws, too!

(Exuberant greetings and hearty hugs are exchanged all around.)

Laurie: You made it down here in good time!

Marty: We wanted to be here to help out however we can.

Grace: (approaching Marty and Chuck) We're so happy to have you, and not just to help!

Walter: (smiling as he looks down the line of sedans parked at the curb) I'm just wondering, are my eyes playing tricks on me, or did you just pull up in three identical cars?

Chuck: (laughing) Three there are, Walter!

Marty: We'll let Mark explain.

(Marty puts her arm around Mark and slips the car keys into his hand.)

Mark: (holds the car keys up as he faces Linda) You're not going to believe this, Linda, but this car is ours, yours and mine! It's a wedding gift from my mom and dad!

Linda: Seriously? I can't believe it!

(Mark and Linda embrace again, and then hug Marty and Chuck, all eyes flooded with tears of gratitude.)

Linda: Thank you both so much!

Michael: And guess who else gets a silver Ford sedan for a wedding gift, Laurie?

Laurie: (looking stunned, her voice filled with emotion) No! You can't be serious! Two cars? Are you kidding?

Chuck: It's true, Laurie. Marty and I talked about what we thought you four would most appreciate before you started graduate school, and we decided the two cars would probably be pretty high on your list.

Laurie: (laughing and then embracing her future in-laws) Pretty high! I'd say at the top of the list! Thank you both so much! I can't think of anything we'd make better use of!

Grace: That's so generous of you. Thank you!

Walter: It certainly is a wonderful and thoughtful surprise! Let's all go into the house and celebrate our kids' good fortune!

(After they all have a chance to unload things from the cars and bring them into the house and into their rooms and take some time to wash up and relax, they sit at the long dining room table to enjoy a lunch of tuna sandwiches and cottage cheese with freshly sliced peaches.)

Mark: God sure has been good to us! Besides getting first-class educations, Michael and I have won the hearts of two beautiful women! I feel like I love everything and everybody right now!

(Everyone can't help but applaud Mark's short, heartfelt speech. Before the tears start rolling again, Walter says a short prayer.)

Walter: Let's pray everybody. *Lord, we are so thankful for our beautiful children, filled with love and gratitude as they are. We wish them much happiness in their marriages and Godspeed in their future educations. And thank you for enabling all of us to be together for this special week of wedding preparation and time together. Thank you, also, for this food. Now let's eat! Amen!*

Everyone: *Amen!*

Walter: After we finish lunch, how'd you all like to take a short drive to see a new subdivision I'm building in Coon Rapids?

Marty: I'd love it! I've always had a keen interest in home design.

(Before anyone can object after lunch, Walter ushers them out the door to their cars, the parents occupying Walter's roomy Buick and the kids loading into one of the silver sedans.)

Walter: (calling to Michael) Just follow me! It's only a short drive from here.

(In no time at all, they pull up in front of a beautiful two-story house, two majestic old oak trees gracing the newly sodded grass.)

Chuck: (gets out of the car and looks around) This is a neat neighborhood, Walter.

Marty: It sure is! And it seems so peaceful!

Walter: I had this house furnished, so I guess you'll be pretty excited about that.

Marty: I'm eager to see it! I'm really interested in interior design.

Walter: (winks at his wife discreetly) Well, in that case, I think you're going to be intrigued by this one, Marty.

(Grace wonders what her husband has up his sleeve because he's built a number of similar-looking houses. Why would this one be any different? When she walks into the house, she immediately sees why it is.)

Marty: Oh my, Walter, these cords lining the walls are sure a new design twist. It's as though this house is built for a blind person.

Walter: (cheerily) Guess what, Marty! It is!

(That immediately gets Mark's full attention. He asks Linda to lead him to one of the walls. She places his fingertips on the cord and he begins following it along the wall. When he comes to a corner and is about to enter another room, he feels a metal plate.)

Mark: (excitedly) It's in braille! It tells where I am and where I'm headed! What a great house!

Walter: Could you picture yourself living here?

Mark: (laughing) Sure, in my dreams, maybe!

Walter: (putting his arm around Mark and beaming) Well, sometimes dreams do come true, Son!

Linda: (excitedly) Dad, what are you saying?

Walter: Well, I thought Mark and you and Michael and Laurie might like to live here while you're going to graduate school at the University of Minnesota. I'd like to extend the offer as a wedding gift.

(The announcement takes everyone by surprise, including Grace. The house has two large master bedrooms, one upstairs and one downstairs, each with connecting studies. A large great room leads to a spacious kitchen, and informational braille is imbedded on plaques near each of the appliances. Glass patio doors lead from the large kitchen to the outside.)

Laurie: (gazing around) Really, Dad? Are you serious?

Walter: Absolutely! What do you think, Mark?

Mark: (smiling) I can't see it, but I think it's an incredible offer! Thank you!

Linda: I love it! Wow! Thank you, Dad!

Michael: I love it, too! I can't believe this is happening! First we get cars and then we get a place to live! Thank you!

Laurie: It's so beautiful! Thank you, Dad!

Grace: (smiles and wraps her arms around her husband) You're a pretty thoughtful guy, you know that?

(On the drive back to the Johnson's house, all the twins can talk about is how fortunate and grateful they are to have parents like theirs.)

Linda: Mark and I were just about to start looking for a place, but having all of us living together in Coon Rapids is just fine with me.

Laurie: Same here. It'll be fun being in the same house. Michael and I will take the upstairs bedroom and study if that's all right with you two.

Linda: That would make it easier for Mark.

Mark: Hey! I could slide down the bannister!

(Everyone laughs.)

NARRATOR: The week whizzes by, and when Saturday morning arrives the Johnson house is buzzing with activity. The wedding is scheduled for 2:30 p.m. in Coon Rapids at the Church of the Epiphany, the Johnson's church, and where Linda and Laurie went to school. It's a walk down memory lane for Marty and Chuck when they enter the church, as they had also had a June wedding many years ago.

Before the Mass begins, the organ begins playing, Grace and Marty wipe away tears, and a beaming Walter walks down the aisle with a radiant bride on each arm. Linda and Laurie are all smiles as their husbands-to-be stand proudly near the first pew. When they reach the front of the church, Walter kisses each of his daughters and embraces them warmly before he hands them off to Michael and Mark, and the young couples move to four kneeling benches positioned in front of the altar.

The Mass begins and a solemn quiet blankets the large church until Holy Communion. The twins receive first, followed by their parents and the rest of the congregation. It takes a long time, as the church is packed with guests. Finally, the four "I do's" are spoken and the couples are pronounced husband and wife!

After the ceremony, everyone gathers in the church reception hall for a delicious luncheon prepared by the women of the parish. It is all very elegant, and the guests enjoy themselves immensely, the last few not leaving until after 6:00 p.m. It has been a happy but exhausting few days for the newlyweds, and they are tired and ready for a relaxing honeymoon at their beautiful new abode. The newlyweds had decided to honeymoon at home, and they can't get there soon enough! They pull up in front of the new house at seven o'clock and sit for a few minutes, admiring it from the outside and talking with one another.

Mark: Something tells me it's going to be real easy adjusting to our new home.

Michael: (boisterously, as he runs toward the house with his new wife clinging to his arm) Well, let's get started! Married life here we come!

Laurie: (laughing as Michael swoops her up into his arms and carries her into the house) Ready or not, here we come!

Linda: (speaking quietly to Mark as she covers his hand with hers and the two of them make their way slowly up the walkway) I get the feeling this is going to be an interesting experience.

Mark: (softly) Yes. I agree. You know all too well that it takes a little getting used to Michael's bursts of energy.

Linda: And Laurie's, but I wouldn't have it any other way!

Mark: (smiling) Me neither. Now, my sweet bride, tell me when we've reached the threshold so your new husband can carry you over!

(Mark soon finds himself exploring every nook of the big new house, room by room. While he's doing that, Michael, Laurie and Linda are in the kitchen, uncorking a bottle of fine white wine.)

Linda: (calling to her new husband) Come join us, Mark! It's time to celebrate!

Mark: (rounding the corner to take part in the festivities) Man this place is cool! I can find my way so easily. Your dad really thought of everything when he planned this house for us.

Michael: (placing a glass of wine in his brother's hand) Well, Mark, you're going to be a "man of words, attorney Mark Dowdle," so how about you making a toast?

Mark: (laughing, as he raises his goblet) More like a man of few words: *Lord, bless our marriages and fill our lives with peace and happiness. Amen.*

Everyone: (clinking their glasses and sipping their wine) *Amen!*

(The couples sit in the living room and talk about the wonder of their new lives, in awe of the fact that they are now married and settling into a beautiful new home.)

Linda: (after a few minutes of amiable chatter) Well, it's getting dark, and it's my wedding night. I'm going to head for the bedroom and see if someone follows.

Laurie: (giggling as she skips out of the kitchen, up the stairway and calls back teasingly over her shoulder) Is anyone coming after me?

Michael: (laughing) Did you hear those two?

Mark: (puts down his wine glass and begins to feel his way along the wall to the downstairs master suite) Hey, I may be blind, but I'm not deaf!

> (When Mark reaches the bedroom and opens the door and enters, the first thing he senses is the aroma of sweet perfume. He follows his nose until he walks straight into the arms of his waiting wife at their bedside. Linda giggles, and Mark holds her close and kisses her tenderly as she begins to slowly undress him. As they climb into bed together, Mark curls up next to her warm body and begins caressing her before engaging in an act of mutual, unimaginable bliss!)

Scene IV: The Honeymoon

NARRATOR: Mark is the first one up in the morning, so he decides to have breakfast ready for everyone by the time they get up. It will be easy, he thinks. However, in his over-confident haste, he makes a wrong turn and crashes straight into the large patio door! Everyone wakes up when they hear the sound of shattering glass. Linda is the first to make it to the kitchen. Mark is standing among the shards of broken glass, blood streaming from his wrist and dripping onto the floor.

Linda: (screaming) Mark! What happened?

Mark: (looking shocked) I don't know!

(Michael and Laurie run into the kitchen)

Michael: (yelling) Oh man! What happened?

Linda: He doesn't know!

Laurie: (quickly examining the gash on Mark's left wrist and wrapping the bloody wound with a hand towel and applying pressure) I think we'd better get you to the hospital!

(Not overly concerned about the bleeding, which he can't see, Mark keeps asking about his wrist as the foursome drives to the Hospital Emergency Room.)

Mark: (excitedly) Do you think I severed a nerve? Will I be able to use my braille machine again?

Linda: We'll see, Mark. We'll see. Take it easy.

(Two hours later Mark's wound has been sutured up at the hospital and everyone is back home.)

Mark: (laughing) I made a bloody mess out of breakfast, didn't I?

Michael: (smiling) You sure did! Why don't you sit down now and try to relax a little, Mark, and we'll all have breakfast together in a minute.

NARRATOR: After they eat, Linda calls her parents and tells them about Mark's mishap. When Walter informs Marty and Chuck, they are upset, but take it all in stride. This won't be the first time one of their sons has come home all bloodied up. However, they do want to see the twins again before heading back to Perham, so after breakfast they all head over to the new house.

Marty: (when she sees Mark with his bandaged wrist) How exactly did it happen?

Mark: I guess I was feeling a little too confident when I left the bedroom. I turned the wrong way and crashed into the patio door.

Walter: (inspecting the door) We're just glad it wasn't a more serious injury. I'll have my men come over and replace the glass today. It'll be just like new.

(After their parents leave, the newlyweds sit and talk

about their exciting morning and the adjustment to their new lives.)

Michael: What would you think about getting a dog, Mark? It would be a useful set of eyes for you, especially for the times when you're alone.

Mark: Might be a good idea.

Linda: I think it would be fantastic!

Laurie: Me, too!

NARRATOR: The foursome doesn't waste any time pondering it further. Several days into Mark's recovery, they are off to the local pound in search of a dog, and as fate would have it, a beautiful three-year-old Golden Retriever named Prince has recently been turned in. Prince was "too much dog" for the elderly couple that owned him. He is an exceedingly attentive and friendly animal, and a breed well known for its intelligence and loyalty. Within the next hour, Michael and Laurie find themselves driving home with Prince sitting happily by an open window next to Mark and Linda in the back seat.

Mark: (enthusiastically) My first job is going to be to acquaint Prince with our house and the neighborhood, and after that we can visit the university campus and let him check it out!

Linda: That's an excellent idea, Mark. We'll have about a month and a half to get used to him and him to us before school starts, so that will give us plenty of time to do some training and have some fun together before we start in on the long school haul.

(Prince is well behaved and very alert on the drive home, taking in all the sights and sniffing constantly out the open window.)

Mark: (exhaling a long breath as they pull up in front of their house) Ah, it's good to be home! I sure hope Prince likes it.

(They head up the front walk, and after Michael opens the door for them, Mark bends down and gives Prince a loving pat.)

Mark: Welcome to your new home, Prince!

(Prince looks up at Mark.)

Linda: He's smiling at you!

Laurie: And wagging his tail!

Michael: (strokes Prince's sturdy back) I'm sure he'll love it here! How could he not?

Mark: (unclips the leash from Prince's collar) Watch and see what he does when I set him free.

(As soon as Mark releases his hand from the collar, Prince

dashes off, wandering from room to room and giving each a thorough sniff test. Shortly after dinner, Linda and Mark snuggle in their comfortable bed and Prince sprawls out contentedly on the furry rug alongside it. It must feel good for him to be out of the pound and in a warm and cozy space with new people who are showing him a whole lot of love.)

NARRATOR: Early the next morning, Laurie and Michael are up early and have breakfast ready by the time Linda and Mark appear with Prince by their side.)

Mark: Prince is hungry, too! I hope you fixed his chow, Michael!

Michael: (places a large bowl of dog food on the floor near Prince) I did! I did!

(Prince scarfs down the food like he hasn't eaten in days.)

Mark: Wow! It sounds like he's starved! They must not have fed him enough at the pound!

Michael: After we eat breakfast, what would everybody think about taking a walk on some of the trails at the Coon Rapids Dam Regional Park?

Laurie and Linda (in unison): Sure!

Mark: I'd love it, and I'll bet Prince would, too!

(Prince does. He's an exuberant and outgoing dog, a large male Golden Retriever who seems ready for anything. He's eager to make friends with everyone, including strangers and other dogs.)

Michael: (after a couple of hours on the trails) Anybody hungry? It's about time for lunch. How about if we drive home and have some sandwiches and then head over to the university with Prince?

Linda: Great idea! Mark and I haven't had a chance to walk around the campus. While we're there we can stop at the bookstore and pick up our class schedules and all of our books.

NARRATOR: After lunch, everyone piles back into the car and they head to the University of Minnesota campus. Prince assumes his favorite spot near the back seat window next to Mark and takes in every detail as they drive along. After they arrive at the campus, they all get out and start walking, first to the Law School, then to the School of Medicine, and next to the School of Nursing. Prince seems to be recording every step of the way with his eyes and nose as they walk from building to building.

Linda: Remember, before we go home we need to stop at the bookstore and get our books and schedules.

Michael: Wow! I'm glad you remembered that, Linda. I forgot all about it!

NARRATOR: After the bookstore stop, everyone is tired and feeling shocked by how much their books cost! When they get home and have a chance to examine them before supper, they all have a lot to share.)

Mark: I think law school's going to be a four-year course in survival tactics!

Linda: (frowning) I got to talk a little to some upper classmen, and they sure didn't offer much encouragement. It sounds like it's going to brutally hard!

Michael: (smiling) It's just the opposite for me. The semester starts with anatomy, histology, embryology, genetics, molecular biology and biochemistry. Easy stuff!

Linda: Wow! Impressive!

Michael: How about you, Laurie?

Laurie: I'll be studying aspects of nursing that aim to improve people's health, and I'll also be doing a lot of hands-on learning when I'm not in the classroom.

Linda: I guess we've all got our work cut out for us. Ready or not, here we come!

ACT IV: WE ARE FAMILY

Scene I: Pregnancy

NARRATOR: Grace calls in October and Linda picks up the phone.

Grace: You kids must be very busy. We haven't heard from you for way too long. How's school going?

Linda: It's been challenging for all of us! The amount of work they're giving us is exhausting!

(Linda sounds tired, and it concerns Grace, so she just chats casually with her for a while.)

Grace: Do you remember what's coming up on November 1st?

Linda: (after a long hesitation) We've been so busy, I completely forgot. Our birthday! I haven't had a minute to think about it.

Grace: And not just any birthday. Your 21st! It's also All Saints Day. Anyway, your dad and I would love to take you all out for a smorgasbord dinner at the Radisson Hotel in

Minneapolis. We hoped if we called soon enough you'd reserve the date for us, unless of course you'd like to spend the day with your husbands, which would be totally fine and understandable.

Linda: It sounds great, Mom! Thank you! I'll ask the gang, but I'm sure Laurie and the guys would love to go. And, Mom, there's something I have to tell you, big news, but it's a secret! Don't say anything to Dad yet!

Grace: You've got me curious. Whatever could it be?

Linda: (laughing) I hope you're sitting down. You're not going to believe this, but Laurie and I missed our periods this month! We think we might be pregnant! Both of us!

Grace: (after an audible gasp) Oh my! Pregnant? Both of you? That is big news! You're right, I can't believe it! (breathing heavily) I'm stunned, and very happy at the same time!

Linda: (cautions her mother) We haven't said anything to Mark or Michael yet, so keep it a secret. Don't say anything to them or Dad. We'll soon know for sure, and if it's true, we'll announce it at our birthday dinner.

Grace: Oh, Linda, I'm so excited! I know Walter and the boys will be, too! It's quite a surprise! We figured you were going to complete your schooling before starting a family.

Linda: (laughing) We did, too, Mom. Seems the rhythm method of natural birth control didn't work so well for either of us. I think your two daughters are soon to be two moms.

Grace: Well, this mom is pretty thrilled hearing she may soon be a grandmother! And, I know Walter will be thrilled as well if he's soon to be a grandfather!

Linda: Okay, Mom, I've got to run. Remember, it's a big secret until we make an announcement at dinner.

Grace: My lips are sealed.

NARRATOR: Halloween arrives and Walter and Grace are kept busy greeting the multitude of trick-or-treaters at their door. Grace can't erase the baby news from her mind as she drops candy into the open bags. She is itching to tell Walter the good news, but true to her word, she doesn't say a thing.

The next day they all meet at the Radisson in downtown Minneapolis. Walter and Grace greet the kids with warm hugs at the front door of the hotel and escort them to the dining room. It's a huge space with elegant table settings and glittering chandeliers. Linda relays the scene in detail to Mark as they make their way to their table.

Michael: The food looks great, Mark! There are hot and cold hors d'oeuvres, a dozen different kinds of cheeses, salads, side dishes, casseroles, roast beef, ham and turkey. You name it, it's here for the taking!

Mark: I'm salivating, ready for round one!

Walter: (after everyone is seated) Well, it's really good to see you kids again. Grace tells me you've all been studying so hard you've lost track of time, you girls almost forgetting your birthday! Tonight we'll just relax and celebrate, so let's begin with a prayer.

(Everyone bows their head.)

Walter: *Dear Lord, you've been so good to us, blessing us with two precious daughters twenty-one years ago. We honor and thank you for letting our daughters meet and fall in love with these two wonderful young men. And we thank you for this bounty of food which we are about to receive. Amen.*

Everyone: *Amen!*

Grace: Okay, let's get this feast started!

(Everyone gets up and heads towards the smorgasbord. The conversation is lively as they start eating and enjoying themselves. Even Prince, who is lying under Mark's chair, is handed an occasional morsel of meat.)

Laurie: (after eating for about fifteen minutes) I'm so stuffed!

Michael: Me, too, but I saw a lot of good-looking desserts!

Walter: Wait just a minute! You didn't think we were going to let this celebration pass without a special cake, did you?

(Walter signals to one of the waiters standing near closed double doors leading to the kitchen, and when they open, another waiter comes through with a large pink-frosted angel food cake held high over his head, the crystal platter deftly balanced on one hand. When he sets it down in the middle of the table, everyone is in awe. Adorned with edible flowers and an elegant: **"HAPPY 21st BIRTHDAY!"** the glowing cake is a sight to behold.)

Linda: (describes the cake to Mark) It's beautiful! Thank you!

Laurie: Wow! It sure is! Thank you!

Linda: (smiles at her sister) It seems like the perfect time to share another reason for celebrating, don't you think, Laurie?

Laurie: I think you're right!

Linda: You do the honors.

Laurie: (clears her throat in dramatic fashion) Okay, before we blow out these candles, Linda and I have special news to share, something big to celebrate in addition to our birthday!

Michael: (laughs) Tell us before the cake burns up!

Laurie: Well…we just found out we're pregnant! Both of us!

(Mark's mouth falls open.)

Michael: (looking stunned) WHAT?

Walter: You're not kidding, are you?

Michael: (disbelief etched on his face) Really? Seriously?

Linda: (reaches for Mark's hand and places it on her belly) It's true. Both of us are pregnant!

Mark: (kisses his wife softly on the cheek) That's not what I was expecting to hear, that's for sure. I can't believe it!

Michael: (wipes the back of his hand across his brow) Wow! Wow! Wow! That's a real stunner! I'm shocked, but I'm very happy! (hugs his wife)

Grace: It's certainly not what you girls had anticipated for this year, but it's wonderful news, and I'm so happy for all of you!

Laurie: Needless to say, the year won't play out quite as planned. We've all got some serious decisions to make.

Walter: This is quite a birthday surprise! Don't worry, girls, you're in good hands and always will be. Having a baby is a grand adventure. Just take things one day at a time. Congratulations to all four of you! Now why don't you take care of those candles before we're all eating a pile of wax!

(While Grace does the honors of serving the cake, the boys sit quietly and reflect on their birthday, which had just been three months earlier, and the fact that all of their lives will soon be dramatically different.)

Walter: (while driving home) It will be alright. They'll just have to make some adjustments.

Grace: I'm sure they will, Walter, but I love them all so much, I just hate to see them struggle.

Walter: Do you remember how little we had when we were newlyweds and you announced you were pregnant?

Grace: I sure do, and we didn't have an education or a nice place to live. We eked out a living and you became a successful builder and here we are!

Walter: I think everyone struggles over this or that when they're starting out. That's just life.

Grace: (sighing) I just don't like to see our kids suffer along the journey, but I guess it's inevitable and will make the easier times more pleasant when they arrive, just like for us. I know it's best not to meddle, better to just wait and watch and be there when they need us and see how it all comes out.

Walter: (chuckling) I agree! You lifted the thought right from my head, honey!

NARRATOR: There isn't much chuckling when the foursome of twins gets home and sit down to talk. Even Prince is affected by the tension. He moves around nervously after eating and is unsettled, not lying quietly in the living room and dozing off as usual.

Mark: Why don't we say the rosary?

Michael: That's a good idea! The four of us have some important decisions to make, and I'm all for praying about them. So, I'll begin. (makes the sign of the cross) *In the name of the Father, the Son, and the Holy Spirit, Amen. I believe in God the Father Almighty....*

NARRATOR: It's getting late by the time they finish the rosary, and everyone is exhausted, especially Linda and Laurie, not only from the fanfare of their birthdays, but also from the whirlwind of emotion surrounding their new status as mothers-to-be. And they can't help but notice the serious attitudes their husbands have developed since learning they're going to be fathers.

Laurie: Why don't we all just go to be bed and get a good night's sleep before we start discussing all of this. I'm pretty tired.

Linda: Good idea. I'm tired, too. We'll all be able to think better in the morning.

Mark: (reaches for Linda's hand) I agree. Let's call it a day.

(As Mark and Linda get up and head for their bedroom, Prince rises and follows close behind. He senses something different has taken place. Life doesn't feel quite as happy and relaxed as it has been, and he doesn't want to miss anything or risk being left behind.)

Scene II: Adjustments

NARRATOR: When they all sit together at breakfast the next morning, it seems a lot of talk has already taken place between Laurie and Michael. They are in a decision-making mode.)

Michael: Laurie and I talked well into the night before we finally got to sleep, and we've decided what we're going to do.

(This startles Mark. He and his brother have always talked things over before making major decisions. Not anymore!)

Michael: We've decided it would be best for us if I quit med school at the end of the first semester and get a job. With a baby, we're going to need a lot more money just to get by, and we need to face reality now before we get any deeper in debt. Laurie will continue with her nursing program until she receives her R.N. in June.

(At first, neither Mark nor Linda knows what to say.)

Linda: We share your concerns, Michael. Mark and I did some talking last night, too. We're all in the same boat. We coasted through St. Ben's and St. John's with scholarships and help from our parents, but now it's a different story. We've been mulling over the idea of dropping out of graduate school at the end of the first semester and getting jobs, too, and now that we know your plan, it seems like a wise choice for us as well.

Mark: (somber-faced as he reaches out to hold Linda's hand) We all have to face the fact that additional income will be a necessity nine months from now.

Michael: Mom and Dad aren't going to believe all we have to tell them.

Mark: I'll write them a letter this afternoon.

NARRATOR: November turns out to be an interesting month. Laurie is saddened by the fact that she will be the only one continuing with graduate school, but will be happy as well if Michael secures a position with a pharmaceutical company and starts working at the end of the semester. His focused science background at St. John's and his *World Book Encyclopedia* selling experience will make him a perfect candidate for contacting doctors and introducing them to new drugs.

The job market isn't quite the same for Linda and Mark. They consider going to work for an insurance company, but the more they think about it and explore the field, the more they know selling insurance is not for them. Things are looking a little dire until the end of the month when they receive a letter from Marty and Chuck, inviting them to come and live with them in Perham until they can get on their feet financially, zero in on their careers, and have the baby.

Mark: What do you think, honey? Would you mind living with my parents?

Linda: (without hesitation) I think it would be wonderful! Your dad said he talked to Mr. Pfenninger, the principal at Perham High School, and he said to tell us that PHS would be having openings in English, World History and Business Law next year, and if we wanted to get teaching credentials and come back there and work, he'd love to have us. He said they'd even create an elective course in Braille if you'd like to teach that, Mark. So, why not! I've never considered teaching as a career, but it might be something we'd both like!

Mark: Well, okay. I'll write them and tell them we're accepting their generous offer.

Linda: I don't know what could be better! Your dad said they'd be looking forward to having Prince be a part of their family, too!

NARRATOR: Marty and Chuck invite Grace and Walter and the twins to their house for Thanksgiving Day, and when it arrives, so does all the company. Grace and Walter show up first, Grace enthusiastically jumping in to help Marty prepare the turkey and all the fixings. The four parents are looking forward to some time to relax and visit with their kids.

Grace: (working busily in the kitchen with Marty) What do you think is going to happen with those kids of ours?

Marty: (assuredly) You know, Grace, I think everything will be okay. They'll work it out. Oh, and by the way, I don't know if Linda mentioned it to you, but we invited Mark and Linda to come and live with us until after the baby's born and they've had a chance to get back on their feet.

Grace: (very surprised) Oh, my! I didn't know! That's very kind of you!

NARRATOR: The Thanksgiving feast goes off without a hitch. There's a lot of laughter and talk about school, work, and babies, and the very real possibility of twins given the double-sided family history of twins. Friday morning everyone is getting ready to drive back to Coon Rapids.

Walter: Chuck, what would you and Marty think about coming to our house for Christmas? By that time the kids will be wrapping up the semester and we can all celebrate their new paths ahead.

Chuck: Sounds great to me!

Marty: It would be lovely! Thank you for the invitation!

NARRATOR: Christmas falls on a Tuesday, and everyone except Laurie will be finished with school. The others will be selling their books back at the bookstore, especially the expensive law books Linda and Mark have purchased.

It doesn't take the kids long to forget about school when Christmas Eve arrives and they pull up in front of the festively decorated Johnson home, hiking through a foot of snow before reaching the front door. Marty and Chuck arrive early from Perham and are happy to help Walter and Grace prepare the holiday dinner. Walter has a blazing fire going and the house is comfortable, warm and cheery.

Walter: (jovially, as the kids arrive) Welcome! Welcome! Merry Christmas to all of you!

> (After a round of hugs and kisses, everyone settles in the living room by the fire and glittering tree to relax and chat and appreciate the array of aromas emanating from the kitchen. The mid-day hours roll by and the festive dinner is soon ready. Table conversation centers on Linda and Laurie and how they've been doing with their pregnancies. The radiant mothers-to-be say they feel fine, and judging by the way Laurie is packing in the food, they wonder if she's eating for three!)

Laurie: (reaches for a second helping of mashed potatoes) Every time I sit down for a meal, I feel like I haven't eaten for days!

Linda: (laughing) Could be a problem if it keeps up for nine months! I don't seem to have the same voracious appetite as you, Sis, but I sure enjoy every bite nonetheless!

Grace: I suppose you girls are taking vitamins and have already seen a doctor.

Linda: I haven't yet, Mom. I figured I'd wait until I get to Perham.

Marty: (smiling) Maybe you could get the same doctor who delivered the boys, Dr. Schoeneberger. He's wonderful! After all these years, he still has his practice in Perham.

Linda: (leans over and kisses a beaming Mark on the cheek) It would be pretty special to have the same doctor who delivered my husband!

Marty: I know you'd love him! Chuck and I sure do!

NARRATOR: After feasting on the delicious Christmas Eve dinner, everyone gathers once again in the living room and begins opening presents. The highlight of the evening is when Linda and Laurie open theirs. They're each handed a small envelope from their dad, but what each contains is huge! The girls open them at the same time and simultaneously withdraw unfolded notes.

Linda: (reads her note) *"To the Children We Love! Walter and I talked about what to get the four of you for Christmas, thought a lot about what life was like for us when we were just* *starting* out. *We decided that you'd probably most appreciate having some extra money just for living. Enjoy! Much love! Mom and Dad."*

(In each of the girls' two envelopes is an even smaller envelope, and the sisters open them slowly together. Within each is a check for $5,000!)

Linda: (mouth falls open) Oh my goodness! Thank you! It's a check for $5,000, Mark!

Laurie: (looks at her check) Dad! Mom! I can't believe this! Thank you! It's $5,000 for us as well, Michael!

(Laurie hugs Michael and tears come streaming down both girls' faces as they move to embrace their parents.)

Michael: That is so generous of you! Thank you!

Mark: (stunned) Yes, thank you so much! We can sure use it!

Laurie: No question about that! Michael and I will definitely put this money to good use.

Linda: The same goes for Mark and me. With our new lives in Perham and a baby on the way, there's no better gift!

(Chuck and Marty join in the hugs of appreciation and gratitude, and the Christmas Eve festivities carry on into the evening hours with more gifts to open and platters of Grace and Marty's home-baked goodies to enjoy.)

NARRATOR: By early January of 1975, the twins' preparation for their new careers takes off. Mark and Linda move to Perham and enroll at Moorhead State Teacher's College to pick up the required education units needed to qualify for teaching positions at Perham High School in the fall. Michael becomes totally immersed in his new job at the pharmaceutical company, spending part of his time in the laboratory and part of it on the road, calling on doctors. Laurie is doing a lot of hands-on work in addition to her bookwork. One day in early spring she just has a yen to talk about it and calls her sister.

Laurie: Hi, Linda!

Linda: Hi, Laurie! What a nice surprise! Is everything okay?

Laurie: Everything's fine, I just felt like giving you a call. How are you doing?

Linda: I'm doing really well, a little tired, but I feel good overall. How about you?

Laurie: I'm still gaining weight like crazy, which doesn't make me very happy, and I have a whole lot of schoolwork to keep up with, but everything's rolling along.

Linda: Have you and Michael decided what you're going to name the baby?

Laurie: Yes, we have! Her name will be Gretchen Marie Dowdle.

Linda: Gretchen Marie! What a sweet name! It's beautiful!

Laurie: How about you and Mark?

Linda: We've decided as well! His name will be William Francis Dowdle.

Laurie: Wow! I love that! It sounds so dignified!

Laurie: And guess what we did at school today?

Linda: What?

Laurie: We practiced giving one another shots and drawing blood.

Linda: Whoa! I wouldn't like doing that!

Laurie: I'm sending a blood sample to my doctor so he can check for any potential problems with the pregnancy. You should do that, too, Sis.

Linda: I'll definitely think about it. Hey, I'm sorry, Laurie, I wish I could talk longer, but I've got to run.

Laurie: That's okay, Sis. It was great to talk to you!

Linda: Likewise! I love you!

Laurie: I love you, too! Bye!

NARRATOR: Not long after Doctor Nelson has checked Laurie's blood sample, he calls her and says he wants her to make an appointment for an amniocentesis procedure for more detailed diagnostic purposes. Of course this concerns Laurie because she knows this procedure is performed to diagnose genetic conditions. She has the procedure a few days later, and Dr. Nelson's office soon gives her a call and asks her to come in for a follow-up appointment to discuss the results. She does so on April 1st, April Fool's Day, a day never to be forgotten!

Dr. Nelson: Good afternoon, Laurie. How have you been feeling?

Laurie: Fine except I think I'm putting on a little too much weight!

Dr. Nelson: (frowning) That's the least of our worries, Laurie. I have the results of the amniocentesis procedure.

(Doctor Nelson can tell Laurie is anxious, so he reaches over, takes her hands in his and looks straight into her eyes.)

Dr. Nelson: Laurie, little Gretchen Marie is going to be born with **Down syndrome**. It means extra challenges, because as

I'm sure you know, a Down syndrome child can have many physical and mental difficulties to overcome. That being said, you're a strong person and I know you'll be a wonderful mother.

(Laurie is shocked! Without saying a word, she rises from her chair and leaves Dr. Nelson's office.)

Michael: (Laurie is sobbing as she enters the house and Michael greets her.) Honey! What's wrong?

Laurie: (falls into Michael's arms as he embraces her) Oh, Michael! It's terrible!

Michael: What's terrible, honey?

Laurie: I just came from Dr. Nelson's office, and he said our baby has Down syndrome!

Michael: (visibly shaken) Oh no! I can't believe it.

Laurie: What did I do wrong, Michael?

Michael: You didn't do anything wrong, honey. Down syndrome just happens when a baby has an extra copy of a chromosome.

Laurie: But what are we going to do?

Michael: I think we'd better start planning because our lives are about to change dramatically. It's no one's fault but God's that this happened, Laurie, and the best answer I can give you is "His will be done."

Laurie: I know you're right. I haven't thought of it that way. It just makes me so sad.

Michael: I feel sad, too. I'm not very hungry. I think I'd like to skip dinner and just go up and crawl into bed.

Laurie: I going to sit here and think about things for a little while, Michael. I'm tired, though. I won't be long.

NARRATOR: After a restless sleep, Laurie and Michael sit down for an early breakfast before getting ready for another day of school and work.

Laurie: I don't know about you, but what happened to me in Dr. Nelson's office yesterday all seems like a bad dream. I'm going to have to call him and apologize for leaving the examining room and office so abruptly. I think I'll call my parents and sister, too, and tell them about our baby having Down syndrome.

Michael: That's a good idea, Laurie. They'll have to learn sometime, and it may as well be now. There's no sense in waiting until she's born.

(Laurie's first call is to Dr. Nelson.)

Laurie: Dr. Nelson, this is Laurie Dowdle. When I saw you yesterday, I was in shock when you told me my baby is going to have Down syndrome. I got up and left without saying a word, and I'd like to apologize for being so rude.

Dr. Nelson: Oh, Laurie, you don't have to apologize. Your response was completely understandable. How are you doing today?

Laurie: I feel better, doctor. Michael and I had a long talk and we've accepted what's going to happen. We're going to begin planning for our new little family regardless of the difficulties a Down syndrome child might present to us.

Dr. Nelson: That's beautiful, Laurie! I think that's the right attitude, and I'm glad to hear that Michael and you have worked it out and are planning ahead. Is there anything else I can help you with?

Laurie: No, doctor, and thanks again.

Dr. Nelson: You're welcome, Laurie. Feel free to call me if you have any more questions.

Laurie: I will. Thank you.

Dr. Nelson: Of course. Goodbye, Laurie.

Laurie: Goodbye, Dr. Nelson.

(Laurie's next call is to her sister Linda.)

Laurie: Hi Linda!

Linda: Hi Laurie!

Laurie: I thought I'd give you a call because I went to Dr. Nelson yesterday and I have some news about our baby.

Linda: What is it? Tell me!

Laurie: Well, we already know it's going to be a girl.

Linda: (somewhat worriedly) Yes….

Laurie: And I already told you we decided to name her Gretchen Marie when you told me that Mark and you are having a boy and naming him William Francis.

Linda: Yes…we both already knew all of that, Laurie. So… what is it?

Laurie: (somberly) Yesterday Dr. Nelson told me that Gretchen Marie is going to be born a Down syndrome child.

Linda: (gasping) Oh no! What are you going to do?

Laurie: We talked. We prayed. We accepted the fact that this will be our new life going forward, and we're planning for it. In the end, Michael and I agreed that it's God's will that has to prevail, not ours, Linda.

Linda: You're right. It's in His hands. You and Michael are a strong and loving couple and I know you'll be amazing parents to little Gretchen Marie.

Laurie: Thanks, Linda. We'll just take it a day at a time and do our best. How are things there?

Linda: We're very busy, but everything's good. We're still both going to Moorhead State Teacher's College to learn to be teachers and doing student teaching at Perham High School. Mark is a natural, and Mr. Pfenninger, the principal, really liked what he saw happening when he visited Mark's classroom. I think Mark's going to be offered a teaching position for next fall. Even if I'm offered one, I think I'll just stay home and take care of the baby, at least for a while.

Laurie: That sounds like a good plan to me, Linda. I just wanted to let you know about Gretchen Marie, but I've got to be going. I haven't told Mom or Dad our baby news yet, and I want to call them. Would you mind breaking the news to Marty and Chuck?

Linda: Of course.

Laurie: Thanks in advance. I love you!

Linda: I love you, too, Sis! Take care! Bye!

(The last call Laurie makes before heading for nursing school is to her mom and dad, Grace and Walter.)

Laurie: Hi, Mom. It's Laurie. I have some baby news to share. Are you sitting down?

Grace: (with concern) What's wrong? Something's wrong. I can hear it in your voice. Why are you crying?

Laurie: Well, I had an appointment with Dr. Nelson, Mom, and he told me our baby is going to be born with Down syndrome.

Grace: (gasps) Oh no! Oh Laurie! I'm so sorry! That's just so shocking.

Laurie: I know, Mom. It put me in shock when he told me, and I just got up and left his office without saying a word. I called him this morning and apologized. Anyway, Michael and I have talked and turned everything over to God and will be planning for our new life together when little Gretchen Marie is born in July.

Grace: (tearfully) She will be a very loved little girl, there's no doubt about that.

Laurie: I'm sorry, Mom, but I have to run or I'll be late for school. I just wanted to let you know. Break the news gently to Dad, if you will. I love you!

Grace: I love you, too, Laurie, and I'll tell Walter. Thanks for letting us know, honey.

(Michael has been patiently waiting for all of the calls to be made.)

Laurie: Okay, Michael, I'm all done and ready to go.

(When Mark comes home from school later than usual on Friday and he and Prince enter the house, their noses begin sniffing aromas which lead them to the kitchen where Linda has started fixing supper.)

Mark: (laughs, breathes in deeply, and begins removing Prince's harness) Something smells fishy in here!

Linda: After I got home from school, Bruno Zanoni stopped by and dropped off some walleyed pike he caught recently. We're having it with fried potatoes and steamed green beans. How does that sound?

Mark: (smiles) Wonderful! I love my wife! Walleyed pike is one of my favorite meals!

Linda: Oh, by the way, Mr. Pfenninger stopped me as I was leaving the building this afternoon and said he wanted to talk to us about next year when we have some time, perhaps early Monday morning before school started.

Mark: When we have some time? He put it that way?

Linda: He did.

Mark: Well, I think we'll have some time just as soon as he does. I want to learn what he has to say!

Linda: And there's one more thing, Mark, some baby news from Laurie, but that's going to have to wait until Marty and Chuck get home for supper.

Mark: Now I'm really curious, and not just about our meeting with Mr. Pfenninger!

(Marty and Chuck get home later from work at the hospital and school and everyone sits down to enjoy the walleyed pike supper.)

Mark: Honey, I think you've got the touch, just like Mom! This walleyed is delicious!

(The talking sort of comes to a halt as everyone eats, and it isn't long before they're finished.)

Linda: Before we have dessert, I have some difficult news to share with all of you about Laurie and Michael's baby. (Linda pauses as her eyes fill with tears.)

Marty: (concerned) Honey, what is it?

Linda: (breathes deeply) She called me today and said that little Gretchen Marie is going to be born with Down syndrome.

(Everyone gasps.)

Mark: No! That can't be!

Linda: I'm afraid it's true, Mark. She just found out yesterday. She and Michael are dealing with the emotion of it all, and Laure asked me to let you all know.

Marty: (tearing up) I'm so sorry to hear it. (long pause) It's not going to be easy, but I know Laurie and Michael will be amazing parents to little Gretchen.

Chuck: (quietly) Yes, they certainly will. She will be very loved.

NARRATOR: Linda and Mark arrive at school early Monday morning, hoping to catch Mr. Pfenninger in his office before school starts, and they do.

Mr. Pfenninger: Come in! Come in and have a seat you two!

(On his desk are two teaching contracts, one for each of them for next year.)

Mr. Pfenninger: I've certainly been happy with your work, and the District would like to offer you both teaching contracts for next year. Linda, you'd be teaching World History and Business Law, and Mark, you'd be teaching 7th, 8th and 9th grade English and two classes for the blind and visually challenged. What do you think?

Mark: (enthusiastically) I think it's a great opportunity to start a career doing something I love doing! Would I still have an aide from the county to transcribe the Braille writing of the students?

Mr. Pfenninger: Yes, you sure would, Mark. This is something new for all of us, and the county sees it as an opportunity to get young people interested in working with and for the blind. How about you, Linda? Have you made up your mind or do you need more time to think about it?

Linda: Well, I feel really good with my pregnancy right now, and I'd welcome the opportunity to teach World History and Business Law, but I think I should hold off for a year.

Mr. Pfenninger: That's probably a wise decision, Linda. When you're ready, we'll have a job for you.

Linda: That's very generous of you! I appreciate your offer, and I'll certainly let you know when I'm ready.

(That night at supper everyone discusses the pros and cons of having a baby and trying to hold down a teaching position at the same time.)

Chuck: I think you made a smart decision, Linda. If you have the baby in July, as predicted, you'd still be nursing, and it would be difficult.

Marty: I think Chuck is right, Linda. It would be pretty challenging. Believe me, it's hard enough taking care of a newborn even when you're not working. And childcare is expensive. My opinion is you'd be better off being at home, but that's for you and Mark to decide.

Linda: (reaches over to Mark and holds his hand) Thanks for talking about it with us. I really appreciate it. What do you think, honey?

Mark: I agree with Mom and Dad, but I'll go along with whatever you feel is best.

Linda: (laughing) Okay, three votes for holding off on teaching until the time feels right! Make that four for four! I'm with all of you! This mama is going to stay home with her baby! I already told Mr. Pfenninger I wouldn't be ready to teach next year, so we're all set.

(Mark and Linda enter Mr. Pfenninger's office early the next morning and Mark hands him his signed contract. Mr. Pfenninger clasps Mark's arm.)

Mr. Pfenninger: Welcome aboard, Mark! And Linda, maybe after the baby's born and you've developed a routine you'll be able to substitute once in a while. Thanks for coming in you two.

Scene III: Birth

NARRATOR: The school year ends on Friday, June 6th, and the kids are eager to get out and start vacationing. Summer has arrived!

Chuck and Mark plan to go fishing Saturday morning, but the plan is canceled when Mark gets a call from his brother Friday night.

Michael: Guess what? We're having our baby sooner than we thought. Laurie went in to see Dr. Nelson today and he said he didn't want to wait any longer. Laurie was already dilated one centimeter, so she's going to be induced on Monday. This Monday! I know this is short notice, but do you think you and Linda could make it down here for the big event with Mom and Dad?

Mark: (enthusiastically) Wow, Brother! This is amazing! Of course, we'll be there! I'll talk to everyone as soon as we hang up, but I expect we'll drive down together tomorrow and be there in time for supper!

Michael: Sounds great! We'll have your rooms ready! We can't wait to see you. Tell Dad to drive carefully. It's a zoo down here with the teenagers out of school and everyone on vacation.

(Marty, Chuck, Linda, Mark and Prince leave Perham after breakfast late Saturday morning, and when they arrive in Coon Rapids, an excited Michael greets them and they exchange hugs.)

Michael: Boy, am I glad you're here! Laurie's in the bedroom. Her water broke about ten minutes ago and she's beginning to have labor pains! Mom, would you go up and talk with her and see what you think?

Marty: Sure.

(Marty is back a few minutes later.)

Marty: (calmly) Michael, it's time to head to the hospital. Call the doctor and tell him you're on your way. While you and Linda are helping Laurie, I'll call Grace and Walter and tell them to meet us there.

(When they get to the hospital, Grace and Walter are already there and are able to talk to Laurie briefly before the nurses whisk her away to be prepped for delivery. About fifteen minutes later, everyone gathers in Laurie's room. This is going to be a new experience for the men. None of them has ever been present for a live birth. Later in the afternoon, Laurie begins having strong contractions, and Dr. Nelson appears and examines her.)

Dr. Nelson: Well, Laurie, we're certainly not going to have to induce you. It looks like it won't be long at all.

(Beads of perspiration form on Laurie's forehead as she breathes heavily and her contractions grow stronger. Michael sits nervously at her bedside, holding her hand and intermittently wiping her face with a cool cloth.)

Dr. Nelson: (begins heading out of the room) I'm going to see a couple of other patients. I'll check on you again shortly.

Laurie: (calling out after Dr. Nelson) I wouldn't go too far, Doctor!

(The nurse and everyone else in the room smiles, but not Laurie. She's serious! She means business! About ten minutes after Dr. Nelson leaves, Laurie's contractions grow more intense, and she tells the nurse it is definitely time for the doctor to return.)

(Dr. Nelson comes back into the room and does a quick examination.)

Dr. Nelson: You're very close! I'm going to do an episiotomy just before the baby arrives, Laurie. That will widen your vagina and cause less damage to the tissues.

(Doctor Nelson injects a local anesthetic. Laure looks crossly at him like he's an alien from outer space. She is having a major contraction and is experiencing pain like never before in her life!)

Dr. Nelson: Keep breathing the way you have been, Laurie, and push real hard during the next contraction!

(Everyone in the room is focused on the drama and excitement of what is about to take place. Linda begins to feel woozy as she watches and has to leave the room, a concerned Mark by her side. Michael does his best to stay calm for Laurie's sake, but is definitely feeling the intensity of the moment. Grace and Marty stand holding hands near the bedside. Walter and Chuck stand side by side a short distance away. They all stare wide-eyed at the scene before them, feeling Laurie's obvious agony and watching the doctor's every move.)

Dr. Nelson: Okay, I'm going to make a small incision now. You won't feel anything.

(Shortly after the incision is made, Laurie makes a strong gasping push and the baby's head emerges, followed by the shoulders, trunk, legs, feet and ten little toes. Dr. Nelson holds up the precious baby girl for Laurie and Michael to see and everyone starts clapping. Laurie's eyes well up with tears as the doctor hands Gretchen Marie to the nurse.)

Nurse: You have a beautiful daughter, Laurie!

(Laurie is overwhelmed, tears streaming down her face as Dr. Nelson begins suturing up her incision.)

Dr. Nelson: You may experience a little pain for a couple of days. It can be relieved with a warm bath or ice packs. I'll give you pain medication to take home in case you need it.

(As Dr. Nelson leaves, he meets Linda and Mark just outside the delivery room.)

Dr. Nelson: Everything went just fine with your sister, Linda. She has a beautiful little girl!

Linda: That's wonderful! Thank you, Dr. Nelson! I'm not feeling dizzy now, Mark. I'd like to go back in the room.

(When they go in, they see everyone crowded around Laurie, congratulating her and Michael on the birth of their daughter.)

Grace: (hugs Linda) Oh, honey, Laurie did so well! Little Gretchen Marie is small, but she's healthy and beautiful!

(Everyone steps aside so Linda can get close to her sister.)

Linda: I'm sorry I wasn't able to hang in there, Laurie. It just became so overwhelming, I thought I was going to faint!

Laurie: (whispers lovingly to her sister) Don't feel bad, Linda. I understand. Are you feeling okay now?

Linda: Much better. I can't wait to see the baby!

Laurie: The nurse said she'd be bringing her back soon.

(No sooner has Laurie spoken than the door to the room opens and the nurse enters carrying a rosy-cheeked newborn swaddled in a nursing blanket. Linda's mouth falls open in awe and her eyes well up with tears when she sees little Gretchen Marie. The nurse approaches Laurie's bedside and very gently places the little bundle into her open arms.)

Nurse: Here's your sweet Gretchen Marie! She weighed in at five pounds, three ounces!

Linda: (moves close to Laurie's bedside) Oh, Laurie, she's absolutely perfect!

(Laurie cradles her baby, and seeing Mark standing alone at a little distance, calls out to him.)

Laurie: Uncle Mark, come closer and meet Gretchen Marie.

(Marty leads Mark to Laurie's bedside. He reaches out his hands and Laurie guides them to the top of the baby's small head. He slides his fingertips ever so gently over the soft fuzz and down the sides of little Gretchen Marie's face, experiencing with his touch what everyone else experiences with their eyes. He slowly withdraws his hands and backs away.)

Mark: Thank you for letting me touch her, Laurie! She's beautiful!

(After everyone has spent some time with Laurie and Gretchen Marie, they leave the room to give Laurie and Michael time to rest and be alone with their little family. It has been a memorable and emotional day, and the new parents are understandably exhausted. Everyone else walks to the parking lot together.)

Walter: Why don't you all drive over to our place for supper. Grace has been planning for this day and we have plenty of food.

(No one has to be asked twice to accept that invitation.)

Linda: I'm hungry!

Mark: Me, too!

(They pull into the driveway. After everyone is in the house, they sit in the living room, munch on hors d'oeuvres and relive the excitement of their day. As soon as Michael arrives from the hospital, Walter uncorks a bottle of chilled champagne and pours a glass for everyone except Linda, who has orange juice.)

Walter: (proudly) Here's to Gretchen Marie Dowdle, our beautiful new granddaughter, and June 7th, 1975, a day we'll always remember fondly!

Everyone: (gleefully as they raise their drinks) Cheers to Gretchen Marie!

Mark: There's another important date coming up very soon!

(Everyone is sipping their champagne, and they look at him quizzically, except Marty and Chuck, who have an idea of what he's going to say.)

Mark: June 9th, this coming Monday, will be Mom and Dad's 24th wedding anniversary!

Walter: (bellowing) You're kidding! Well, we're going to have to celebrate that, too!

(Before anyone can interject, Walter begins planning the activities.)

Grace: (smiling) Not so fast, dear. Perhaps Marty and Chuck already have plans that involve just the two of them.

Marty: (smiling) We certainly don't want to wear out our welcome. We were planning to stay until after the baby was born and then head home.

Grace: I'm guessing Laurie will be coming home on Monday. Would you like to celebrate your anniversary with your new granddaughter? We'd love to have you stay with us an extra couple of days if you can!

(Marty and Chuck talk it over and agree there is probably no better way to celebrate their anniversary than to share it with family, so they decide to stay. After a delicious supper of cold chicken, potato salad, hot buns, dill pickles and fresh tomatoes from the garden, Grace goes to the kitchen and returns with a beautiful pie.)

Michael: You're going to love the dessert Grace made, Mark! It's a lemon meringue pie, and the peaks of the meringue are slightly browned just like Mom makes!

Mark: (a big smile breaks over his face) I can already taste it!

(After everyone has had their fill, they gather in the living room and say the Joyful Mysteries of the Rosary in thanksgiving for all the gifts God has given them. Even Prince seems thankful and happy to just lie there during the hubbub and gnaw on a large bone Walter gave him. The next morning everyone meets at the Church of the Epiphany in Coon Rapids for Sunday Mass, and after Mass they all drive to the hospital to see Laurie and the baby. They are both doing fine.)

Laurie: The doctor says I can go home tomorrow!

Grace: That's great! We're all so thankful everything went so well. We'll have everything ready, and you'll have extra hands to help, experienced hands! Marty and Chuck are staying an extra day so we can all celebrate your homecoming and their wedding anniversary together. It just happens to be June 9th!

NARRATOR: Laurie is discharged from the hospital early Monday morning, and Michael takes the day off from work so he can be home. Laurie starts breastfeeding Gretchen Marie in the hospital, and mother and daughter are doing just fine as they drive home.

Laurie: She's such a little sweetheart, Michael!

Michael: She sure is! And a good sleeper, too!

Laurie: Let's hope it lasts!

Michael: I'm sure it will, honey! You're going to be a great mother!

Laurie: I hope so!

NARRATOR: The double celebration takes place as planned. Laurie and Michael are happy, but tired, when everyone leaves and they can get settled into a routine of diaper changing and breastfeeding with little Gretchen Marie. The only problem is that the baby is having trouble sleeping since coming home, and both parents are feeling exhausted when Linda calls two months later.

Linda: Hi, Laurie! How are you doing?

Laurie: Oh, Sis, it's a new experience, that I can tell you! Gretchen Marie doesn't like to sleep very much, and I'm tired!

Linda: I guess we're both in a fix, you with little sleep and me with an overdue baby! Here it is, July 31st, and I keep getting bigger. The doctor says he'll give me another week and then he'll have to induce labor. We'll see! I have a hearty appetite and I feel good, but I sure am ready! It's so interesting how we all entered graduate school without a thought about having babies, and now here we are, one already born and another on the way. It sure is different from St. Benedict's and our courting days!

Laure: (laughing) That's for sure!

Linda: I can hear baby Gretchen crying. Call me whenever you have some free time, Sis. If you have any tips for me before William Francis is born, let me know what they are. I love you!

Laurie: I love you, too, Linda! Keep me posted and I'll call you soon! Bye!

NARRATOR: Linda didn't have to wait much longer after she talked to Laurie. William Francis Dowdle arrived early Friday morning on August 8th, 1975. He was a big baby, eight pounds, six ounces! Mark didn't go to work that day and both sets of proud grandparents were at the hospital as well, eager to relish the birth of their second grandchild .

When William Francis was all cleaned up and brought to Linda and she cuddled him and began breastfeeding him, Mark leaned down to kiss his son's fuzzy little head. It was precious to behold, a newborn son intent on his mother's milk and a new father intent on loving his son!

Scene IV: The Downward Spiral

NARRATOR: Laurie and Linda give birth to Gretchen Marie and William Francis and decide to stay home with their babies; Michael is busy calling on doctors and working in the laboratory for Minneapolis Pharmaceuticals; Mark is beginning his first year of teaching Braille and English at Perham High School; Walter, Grace, Chuck and Marty are inching their way towards retirement.

By early September, Mark and Linda establish a smooth routine of caring for their newborn son, and on Monday, September 8th, school begins. Mark's first two classes are Braille, third period is prep, and after lunch he has 7th, 8th and 9th grade English. His classroom is like all the others, high ceilinged, large, square iron radiators along one wall, and space enough to accommodate forty desks. The room is painted a pastel pink, which, of course, doesn't make any difference to Mark.

(The bell rings for first period and the kids begin entering Mark's classroom. Mark stands in the hall with Prince to greet them, and a big kid carrying what looks like a small suitcase comes hurrying down the hall. He's making a clicking sound with his mouth.)

David Overton: Good morning, Mr. Dowdle! My name's David Overton. I'm a new student here and I'm in your class.

Mark: (looks in the direction of the voice) Good morning, David! Thanks for introducing yourself. We're happy to have you!

David: Where do you want me to sit?

Mark: (steps into the classroom for a moment) Would one of you please show David Overton his desk?

Joey Gentilli: I will, Mr. Dowdle.

(Joey leads David to his desk, and David immediately takes his Braille typewriter from its case, sets it up on his desk and is ready to go to work. Then Joey approaches Mark, who is standing near the door.)

Joey: (whispering) Mr. Dowdle!

Mark: Is that you, Joey?

Joey: Yes!

Mark: What is it, Joey?

Joey: I know you couldn't see him, but that new guy, David Overton, is not only blind, he doesn't even have eyeballs!

Mark: Thanks for telling me that, Joey.

(The second bell rings and Mark enters the room and stands at the front of the class next to his desk with Prince alongside him, facing the students.)

Mark: Good morning, class. My name is Mr. Dowdle, and I'm guessing some of you have seen me around town before. I was born in Perham and attended grade school and high school here. It's good to be back, and I'm glad so many of you signed up to learn braille. I'm excited to be your teacher! Before we begin, you'll notice there are two rectangular cards on each desk. They each have your first and last names, and one of them is in braille. If you haven't already, please move around until you're seated in the desk that has your printed name on the card. That's the seating chart I'll be using, and it will be a big help in getting to know all twenty of you. It may seem a little unusual for you to see a dog in the classroom, but Prince here is my partner and friend, and in no time at all I'm sure he'll be your friend, too. So, let's begin by my answering any questions you may have. Just speak right up, and tell me your name first so I can begin recognizing your voice. This will obviously be different than other classes where you raise your hand before speaking. Okay, any questions?

Ken Anderson: Mr. Dowdle, my name is Ken Anderson. I was wondering if you'd mind telling us a little more about yourself so those of us who don't know you or didn't know you when you were living in Perham can get to know you better.

Mark: I think that's a good idea, Ken. Thanks for asking. I'll make it brief, and then each of you can tell me about yourselves. I think it will be an excellent way to spend our first class together. So, I was born in Perham in August of 1953, and I have a fraternal twin brother. I'm Mark and he's Michael. We both graduated from Perham High School and St. John's University in Collegeville, Minnesota and are married to identical twin sisters! My wife Linda and I have a new baby boy, William Francis Dowdle, born just four weeks ago!

My brother and I were born prematurely and were very small. We were given oxygen in the hospital to help us survive, and unfortunately that caused me to develop a condition called retinopathy of prematurity, which caused total blindness when I was just a toddler. It has never held me back in any way. My brother and I did pretty much everything together when we lived in Perham, including running track and riding our tandem bicycle all around town. Shortly after I got married, I had the good fortune of adopting Prince from a dog pound in Minneapolis, and he's been my eyes and loyal companion every moment since.

(Mark reaches down and pats Prince.)

Mark: That's the short version of my tale. Now it's your turn. How about starting us out, Ken?

(Ken stands and isn't shy at all telling about himself, and when he finishes, the other nineteen students do likewise.)

Mark: (smiling) Thank you for that! I really appreciate knowing more about each of you.

(Prince lets out a big yawn and the class laughs.)

Ken: This is Ken Anderson again, Mr. Dowdle.

Mark: Yes, Ken.

Ken: Your dog just gave us a huge yawn!

Mark: (laughing) I guess Prince doesn't appreciate what you told me about yourselves as much as I do. Before the bell rings, let me give you your homework assignment. I want you to run your fingertips over the raised dots on the card on your desk. As I've told you, that's your name spelled in braille. See if you can recognize those letters in any order with your eyes closed by the time you come to class tomorrow. And, David Overton, because you already know how to read and write in braille, please write a detailed version of your life for me, especially what caused you to be blind. I think you're going to be my teaching assistant.

(The bell rings and Mark's classroom empties quickly as his students rush out to their next class. Mark does a repeat performance with his second period class, the bell rings, and his braille students are out the door to their third period classes. Mark stands and grasps Prince's leather handle.)

Mark: (spoken with a sigh of relief) Well, Prince, two down, three to go! It's our prep period. Let's you and me head out for a walk and bathroom break.

(On their way down the hall, Mark meets Principal Pfenninger, who stops and identifies himself.)

Mr. Pfenninger: Well, Mark, how's it going so far?

Mark: I think I'm going to like teaching. Prince and I got off to a great start with my first two braille classes. Now we're off for a walk before lunch and my afternoon English classes.

Mr. Pfenninger: Good for both of you! We're lucky to have you here!

(The principal leaves for the cafeteria, and the lunch break is an hour. Mark walks home with his dad for lunch.)

Chuck: How'd it go, Mark?

Mark: I feel like it went really well. From what I could hear, I think they're going to enjoy learning braille, and if my first two classes are any indication, I think I'm going to like working with students. I hope my afternoon English classes go as smoothly.

Chuck: I'm sure they will. All you have to do is be yourself. That's what the kids want. You respect them, and they'll respect you. Don't think for a minute they can't sense if you enjoy teaching and like being around them. They can! Now let's pick up the pace and get home to lunch!

(Linda is cuddled on the couch with William Francis when Chuck and Mark come home.)

Linda: (enthusiastically) How'd it go?

Mark: Really well! I think I'm going to like teaching!

Marty: (calls out from the kitchen) I'm listening! I'm just getting some lunch for you.

(Monday's lunch was often made from Sunday's dinner leftovers, in this case sandwiches with thinly-sliced roast beef on white bread with iceberg lettuce and a lot of mustard, just the way Chuck and Mark liked them.)

Linda: I don't see how you two can even taste the roast beef with all that mustard!

(Chuck and Mark just laugh and keep on eating.)

Chuck: (on the way back to school with Mark) You're going to experience quite a difference between your 7th, 8th and 9th grade English classes when you meet with them this afternoon. Just listen closely, and you'll see what I mean.

(As the 7th graders make their way into Mark's classroom and walk past Prince, Mark notices that most of their voices are high pitched, boys and girls alike, especially compared to the voices of his morning classes. Of course, that is because the Braille students are 9th graders. The bell rings and Mark rises from his desk and faces his students.)

Mark: Good afternoon, class. My name is Mark Dowdle, I'm happy to be your English teacher this year, and this is my friend, Prince.

(Mark no sooner finishes introducing himself and Prince when the door opens and a flushed, sweaty, out-of-breath young boy rushes into the room. The students start laughing, and Mark immediately senses what's happening. He looks towards the door.)

Mark: Welcome, my friend! My name is Mr. Dowdle, and this is my dog, Prince. It's our first day back to school, so don't worry about being a little late. Your name is on a card on your desk, so when you find it, have a seat and I'll begin class.

(It doesn't take the boy long. There is only one empty desk among the forty in the classroom.)

Mark: I have a seating chart on my desk, so when any of you speak, if you first tell me who you are, I'll try to remember your name and where you're sitting. Listening is the key! When I give directions, you're going to have to get them the first time. They won't be repeated. This first week of school we're going to read a good book to get you back into the habit of reading. The name of the book is *A Long Way to Go*. It's a story about three kids on vacation with their parents. The kids are six, eight and ten years old, and they're spending the day in a supervised childcare program at a Florida resort hotel until their parents return. The problem is that at the end of the day, their parents don't return to pick them up. What would you do if you were one of those kids? As you read this book, I want you to be thinking about problems that may have happened with your family, because at the end of the week that's what your writing assignment is going to be, to compare your family to the family in *A Long Way to Go*. Now, if one of you will hand out the books on the shelf by the windows, we can get started, and you may have the rest of the period to read.

(About five minutes before the bell rings, Mark has the students return the books to the shelf. Some of them are so engrossed that they're still trying to read it on the way to the shelf. The bell rings and the 7th graders leave the room, running to their next class, and the 8th graders begin filing in slowly. Mark gives the same directions to the 8th and 9th graders as he gave to his 7th graders, with the exception that each grade is given a different book to read.)

Mark: So, let's get started. The book you're going to read is *The Diary of a Young Girl*, written by a young girl whose name is Anne Frank. She's a thirteen-year-old Jewish girl who flees with her family from their home and hides in a small attic apartment behind her dad's business for two years to avoid being taken to a concentration camp by the Nazis during World War II. It must have been a terrifying experience and certainly challenging to hide for so long in a small space with a family, but they had no choice, as their lives depended on it. How many of you think you could survive such a thing for two years? I don't think I could. What's in this book is true. It really happened! So, let's get started reading!

(Once the 8th graders started reading, you could have heard a pin drop in the classroom, it became so quiet. And when it was time to return their books to the shelf, they were reluctant to do so, but they did. They sauntered out the door as the veteran 9th graders made their way in, tired from having to spend their first day back at school after a relaxing summer.)

Mark: It's good to have you all back after spending such a relaxing summer, and I know you must be tired after already attending five of your classes, so let's get started this week by just kicking back and reading a good book. The title of the one I picked out for you is *To Kill a Mockingbird* by Harper Lee. I think you're going to enjoy it, and I think it's going to get you thinking. It's a serious novel, compassionate, dramatic and deep. *To Kill a M*ockingbird is about accepting others in spite of their differences. What happens when racism raises its ugly head in a small Southern town is one of the questions you're going to have answered by the time you finish this book, and as you read it, remember to keep comparing your family to the one in the book because that's what you're going to be writing about at the end of the week. So, let's get started and enjoy it!

(It's so quiet Mark can hear the fluttering of pages shortly after the reading begins. "This is too good to be true!" he thinks. Once again the minutes pass quickly and the 9th graders seem engrossed in the book, and they're 9th graders, so shortly before the bell rings, Mark asks if they'd like to take their books home to read. He hears a chorus of yesses, and that answers his question. He can't see it, but some of the students are holding their books open and still reading as they leave the room.

That night at supper, the table talk isn't about how Marty's day had gone at the hospital nor how Linda cared for William Francis all day at home, and not about how Chuck's day had gone at school with his 10th, 11th and 12th grade English classes. It's about how Mark had fared with his classes.)

Mark: Boy! I have a whole new appreciation for your work, Dad. Being totally in charge is quite different than student teaching where you have a master teacher to rely on in case you need help.

Chuck: It's pretty neat you recognize that, Mark, and I'm sure you'll gain an even fuller appreciation the longer you teach. I'd say we all have important jobs, especially our gals. It looks like they're ready for us to chow down, so let's pray.

Mark: If it's okay with you, I'd like to say grace tonight, Dad.

Chuck: Please do.

Mark: *Father in heaven, we thank you for showering our families with your many gifts! Thank you for your love and care of Mom and Dad and Linda! Thank you for our beautiful son! Thank you for my first day of successful teaching! And thank you for this food! Amen!*

Everyone: *Amen!*

(Linda leans over and kisses Mark on the cheek.)

Marty: Very nice, Mark.

Chuck: (smiling) Way to keep it short, Son! The aroma of that fried chicken is making me delirious!

(Everyone begins eating.)

Linda: So, Mark, tell us more. How did it go?

Mark: It felt pretty good! The students in my two morning braille classes were enthusiastic and ready to learn. In the afternoon it's all English, three in a row, 7th, 8th and 9th graders. I'm getting to experience the whole range of junior high kids. It feels rewarding already, and it's only the first day! And, Dad, you'll be happy to know I got all three classes reading like crazy the first day!

Chuck: Good work, Mark. Keep it up!

Marty: Sounds like everything went really well, Mark. They sure are lucky to have you.

Mark: Thanks, Mom, and I feel lucky to have them.

Linda: How did Prince do?

Mark: He was the perfect teacher's assistant, and he soaked up a whole lot of attention from the kids! (reaches down and scratches Prince's head) It was quite a first day for both of us. How about you, Mom? How'd your day go?

Marty: It was enjoyable as always, but not nearly as exciting as yours. You all know about mine. Let's hear how your wife's day went with my adorable grandson!

Linda: It was wonderful! William Francis is such a good little baby. It was a day of eating and sleeping and a whole lot of cooing. The hours flew by. I sure am enjoying being a mother!

Mark: (smiles at his mom and reaches out to hold Linda's hand) And you two mothers don't come any better!

(The peace and joy is broken when a demanding cry is heard from down the hallway.)

Linda: (rises from her chair) Could be a dirty diaper or a hunger cry!

Mark: (laughs and stands) Or both! We'd better double up on this one!

(Chuck and Marty remain seated and keep eating.)

Chuck: I bet that makes you think of old times.

Marty: It sure does, although we were living in a basement apartment when it happened, not in a big, bright house like this!

Chuck: It sure is nice to be able to help the kids get off to an easier start.

Marty: I'll say. The basement apartment was comfortable, and memorable to say the least, but if I'd had a choice, I would have much preferred to live above ground with the twins.

(Linda comes out with William Francis cuddled in her arms and nursing. Mark follows close behind.)

Mark: It was a double whammy!

(Everyone laughs.)

Linda: (smiles down at William Francis, sucking as if his life depends on it) This boy likes to eat as much as his dad, and he definitely had dirty diapers!

Mark: (throws his head back and theatrically breathes in a large draught of fresh air) He sure did! I may not be able to see him, but I sure can smell him! (Everyone laughs.)

(After the dishes are done, everyone relaxes out on the back patio. It's still warm in the house, and a welcoming breeze causes the leaves on the trees to flutter. As the sunlight filters through, William Francis seems hypnotized by their movement. He coos constantly while Mark holds him in his arms and gently rocks him.)

Mark: This is the best time to hold William Francis, when he's clean, fed and happy!

NARRATOR: Tuesday morning arrives and Mark is ready. How could he not be? He's thought a lot about his approach to his second day of classes.

Mark: Well, how many of you were able to learn your names in braille last night?

(All twenty hands shoot up, but Mark doesn't hear a response.)

Mark: Was it that hard?

Colleen Belka: Colleen Belka, Mr. Dowdle. All of us just raised our hands. We forgot that you couldn't see.

Mark: Thanks, Colleen. I know this way of interacting takes some getting used to. So, let's get started on our next assignment. The first thing I'd like you to do is exchange your braille name card with that of another student. Once you've done that, close your eyes and run your fingers over the raised dots and practice reading your fellow student's name.

(Everyone exchanges name cards and the room becomes quiet as the students go to work. Mark leans forward and gives Prince a gentle loving stroke and then calls David Overton to his desk and hands him a "B" volume of the Braille edition of the *World Book Encyclopedia* to read. After fifteen minutes, Mark hears his students beginning to talk quietly with one another.)

Colleen: Colleen Belka, Mr. Dowdle. I had Laurie Hertel's name, and it was pretty easy. Our names have some of the same letters, so I had a head start.

Mark: That's what you're going to find, Colleen. You'll often be encountering repeated letters, so the more you practice, the easier braille will become for you to read. One of the things we'll be doing in this class is reading from the Braille edition of the *World Book Encyclopedia*. I'm going to ask David Overton to read the Braille article from the encyclopedia to you because he already knows how to read braille and is a real pro. When David reads, you'll see his fingers moving very quickly. It takes time to learn; the important thing is to be patient and not give up! Okay, David!

(The students watch David's every move as he navigates his way to the Braille article and begins to read aloud.)

David: "*Braille is a code consisting of small raised dots on paper, dots that can be read by touch. Louis Braille, a 15 year-old blind French student, developed a raised dot reading system in 1824. The idea came to him from the dot code punched on cardboard used by Captain Charles Barbier to send night messages to his soldiers.*

"*In 1829, Braille published a dot system based on a 'cell' of six dots. From the 63 possible dot arrangements, Braille worked out a complete alphabet, punctuation marks, numerals, and, later, a system of writing music. His code was at first not officially accepted for all written languages and for mathematics, science and computer notation.*

"*People who are blind read braille by running their fingers along the dots. They can write braille on a six-key machine called a Braillewriter, or with a stylus on a pocket-sized metal or plastic slate. Braille books are pressed from metal plates. The characters are stamped on both sides of the paper by a method called interpointing. Dots on one side of the page do not interfere with those printed on the other. In the early 1960's, publishers began using computers to speed up production of braille books. Text typed into the computer is automatically translated to braille. The computer transfers the raised braille figures onto paper or metal plates for use in a press. By an alternative method, a vacuum braille-former duplicates hand-transcribed braille pages onto plastic sheets which are then bound in volumes."*

Mark: Well, class, there you have it, reading about braille from a Braille encyclopedia, and read very expertly by your fellow classmate who is blind, David Overton!

(The class cheers and applauds for David, and Mark listens as the students share their enthusiastic reactions.)

Mark: We'll begin studying the braille alphabet and punctuation, and as soon as you think you're ready, you may begin reading articles from the Braille *World Book Encyclopedia* just like David did today. I'm going to ask Rose Hammers to hand out paper copies of the braille alphabet. Keep them and study them with your eyes closed, and you'll soon be reading braille.

(The students quietly study the braille alphabet until the bell rings. They leave and the second period braille students start to file in. Linda Hertel is the first person to enter the classroom.)

Linda Hertel: Good morning, Mr. Dowdle! Linda Hertel!

Mark: (turns his head in her direction) Just a minute, Linda. That name's familiar. I believe I just had a Hertel girl in my first period braille class.

Linda: You did! That's my identical twin sister Laurie.

Mark: You're kidding! Laurie and Linda? Those are the names of the identical twins my brother and I married!

Linda: Really? Wow! What are the odds of that happening?

Mark: (laughing) Pretty slim, I'd say! Linda, would you mind taking roll for me today?

Linda: I'd be happy to, Mr. Dowdle!

(Mark follows the same routine he did with his first period braille class, except he reads the Braille article aloud from the *World Book Encyclopedia* because there's no David Overton to help him. He finishes the article.)

Mark: Are there any questions?

Carol Fisk: Carol Fisk, Mr. Dowdle. How long have you been reading braille?

Mark: (smiling) Many years, Carol. It all started when my dad was teaching at Perham High School and selling *World Book Encyclopedia* during the summers. *World Book* began publishing their encyclopedia in braille, and my dad was lucky to acquire a free set for the school. I was young at the time and took to reading braille like a fish to water! The complete set is still at the school in the library, and any of you are welcome to read articles from it as soon as you learn to read braille. So, let's get hot on that alphabet and make it happen!

Carol: Thanks, Mr. Dowdle. I'll definitely do that!

(The braille alphabet is handed out and the students study diligently until the bell rings.)

Mark: (quietly to himself) Wow! Where did the minutes go, Prince? I'm going to have to learn to manage my time better, and you deserve a breather.

(Mark could sense Prince's joyful anticipation as he attaches his harness and they head out the door towards home for lunch. Before Mark knows it, he's standing in front of his fourth period 7th grade English class.)

Mark: We're going to continue reading aloud from *A Long Way to Go* today and Wednesday, and we'll see how far we get. I'd like to finish the book on Thursday so we have some time to talk about it and get ready to write for your grade on Friday. Be thinking about how your family compares to the one in the book. Okay, who would like to start out?

Janice Stollenwerk: Janice Stollenwerk, Mr. Dowdle. I would!

Mark: Okay, Janice. Thank you!

(Once Janice starts reading, there is no stopping her, and she is an excellent reader.)

Mark: Thanks, Janice! Well done! Now let's have Jerry Theodorson read, followed by Dale Witzke, and when he gets tired, others in the class can take over.

(The minutes roll by and the students find themselves engrossed in the story. A few minutes before the bell rings, Mark interrupts and has the books collected.)

Mark: A lot has happened in the story since yesterday. Who would have thought those kids would take off from the hotel just like that?

Leroy Rosenthal: Leroy Rosenthal, Mr. Dowdle. I would have done the same thing!

Mark: Well, Leroy, kids are curious, that's for sure! They're only going to sit in a hotel room for so long. To sum it up, Ashley and Brett are wondering why their parents haven't returned to the hotel, and six-year-old Shane is shocked when she learns her mom and dad are still gone. The kids are all afraid of what the hotel people are going to do with them if their parents don't return, so they take off and try to get home by themselves, but, the hotel manager spots them and brings them back.

Jean Wendt: Mr. Dowdle, Jean Wendt. I was happy when the kids escaped from the hotel again after their parents didn't show up, but I wondered if they were going to be harmed when they met that Birdwoman. She was really weird! I thought she was going to call the police and turn the kids in, but when she encouraged them to go home and not let people stop them no matter what, I knew she was in favor of what they were trying to do and was going to help them.

(The bell rings and the 7th graders are up and out the door in a flash.)

Mark: (reaches down and gives Prince a scratch) Wow! Do you think we can keep up this pace, Prince?

(Mark can hear Prince's tail thumping exuberantly on the floor.)

Mark: You're right, Prince. Of course, we can! Of course, we can!

(And they did. The 8th graders entered the room and didn't wait for someone to pass out copies of *The Diary of a Young Girl*. They went and picked them off the shelf themselves.)

Lorraine Leuders: Lorraine Leuders, Mr. Dowdle. Can we read to ourselves, today?

Mark: Why's that, Lorraine?

Lorraine: Because having to listen to someone reading aloud is boring, and besides, we can read faster if we read to ourselves.

(Class chuckles. Mark is amused by Lorraine. He appreciates the fact that she isn't afraid to let him know just what she thinks.)

Mark: I can understand how you feel, Lorraine. How do the rest of you feel about reading to yourselves?

(Mark can hear murmurs of support from around the room.)

Mark: Okay, you've convinced me! Carry on by yourselves!

(The room falls silent as the students find their places in the book and begin reading. In what seems like no time at all, the bell rings, the eighth graders are gone, and the ninth graders saunter in and are already in their seats.)

Mark: This is only my second day of teaching and I've already learned a lot. Number one is students get bored going over old stuff, and number two is students prefer to read to themselves like you did yesterday. So, the hour is yours.

(The two braille classes worked on the alphabet the rest of the week. The English classes read silently Wednesday and were allowed to take the books home to finish them that night so they could be discussed Thursday. Early Thursday morning, Prince and Mark were already in the classroom, getting ready for the first period braille class to arrive. Ninth grader, Joey Gentilli, who was in two of Mark's classes, entered the room.)

Joey: (speaking in a soft voice) Good morning, Mr. Dowdle. It's Joey Gentilli. I'm in your first period braille class and last period English.

(Mark was a little surprised. Almost a whole week had gone by and he had rarely heard Joey's voice.)

Mark: Good morning, Joey! What brings you here so early?

Joey: I wanted to talk to you about what happened in the book we're reading.

Mark: Sure, Joey!

Joey: Well, it really bothered me the way Boo Radley was treated just because he was different. Why does that have to happen to people, Mr. Dowdle?

Mark: (shaking his head) I don't know, Joey. That's a hard question to answer, but a good one to ask. It would be interesting to discuss it in class this afternoon.

Joey: (very softly and almost in a whisper) Please don't mention that I was the one who brought it up, Mr. Dowdle.

Mark: Don't worry, Joey. I won't.

(As Mark's first period braille students file into the room and begin working on their alphabets, Mark can't help but wonder why Joey Gentilli is so sensitive about the way Boo Radley is treated in *To Kill a Mockingbird.* What Mark can't see and what Mark doesn't know is that Joey Gentilli has a severe cleft palate, which has left his lip very deformed. Mark knows that Joey speaks with a slight lisp, but he doesn't know that Joey has been teased about his lip for a long time by students and even his mother and older sister at times.)

Mark: Good morning, class! After the alphabet, I wasn't sure you were going to show up today! Keep working on it, and when you think you have it mastered you can begin working on some Dolch Basic Sight Words. These are bread and butter words that make up about ninety per cent of a person's reading.

Joey: Mr. Dowdle, I think learning the braille alphabet is really hard!

(Mark recognizes Joey's voice immediately, but is surprised to hear him speak out.)

Mark: Well, that's to be expected, Joey. Learning to read braille isn't easy! It takes determination and a lot of practice. You'll catch on over time, but not likely as fast as someone who's blind and doesn't have any visual distractions. I think you'll find it helpful to close your eyes while you're learning.

Joey: Thanks, Mr. Dowdle.

Mark: Okay, let's get started.

NARRATOR: Thursday afternoon, discussions begin in each class about the three books Mark had his 7th, 8th and 9th graders read. Most of the 7th graders talked about all of the obstacles the kids met before they finally made it home and found out that their parents had been in an accident. It was different with the 8th and 9th graders.)

Mark: Do any of you have any thoughts you'd like to share about *The Diary of a Young Girl?*

Sharon Rosen: Sharon Rosen, Mr. Dowdle.

Mark: Yes, Sharon.

Sharon: I would hate to be cooped up like that with grown-ups for two years!

(Everyone chuckles.)

Sharon: I guess if my life depended on it, I'd be able to do it.

Mark: That was certainly true for Anne. She had no choice.

Judy Mondt: Judy Mondt, Mr. Dowdle. It was so interesting the way Anne revealed all her personal confidences to Kitty, everything that was on her mind and in her heart. It's fascinating, especially since she was thirteen like me.

(The girls in the class nod their heads in agreement.)

Mark: I can sure understand how that would make it even more intriguing. How about you boys? What are your thoughts about it?

Charles Meyer: Charles Meyer, Mr. Dowdle.

Mark: Yes, Charles. What do you think?

Charles: It was interesting how the Franks and all those other people went into hiding to escape from the Nazis. It made me think about how much families had to deal with during the war.

Mark: You're right on that, Charles. Just think how terrifying it must have been. They had to tolerate an extraordinary amount just to survive, and, of course, there were a large number who didn't make it!

(The class rolled by as the students asked more questions and shared their thoughts. Mark enjoyed every minute of lively, impromptu discussion.)

Mark: I'd like to remind you to be thinking about comparing your families to the ones in *The Diary of a Young Girl* because that's what you'll be writing about tomorrow for your grade.

(The bell rings and one more class to go, the 9th graders.)

Mark: Well, it'll be payday tomorrow because you already know you'll be writing about how the family in *To Kill a Mockingbird* compares to yours.

(The ninth graders look around at one another, reactions ranging from smiling to frowning. They were being asked to reveal something not only about themselves , but also about members of their families. Mark was surprised when he heard Joey Gentilli's voice.)

Joey: Won't that get a little personal, Mr. Dowdle?

Mark: Perhaps. It's just a regular compare and contrast writing assignment. How much you choose to reveal is totally up to you. It's a good way for me to get to know all of you better, but I don't want anyone to feel uncomfortable. Your family comparison, regardless of the level of depth you choose, will also help to demonstrate your understanding of the roles Atticus, Scout and Jem played in the book.

(Had Mark been able to see Joey's face, he would have realized his explanation provided little reassurance for him. Remembering Joey's concern for how Boo Radley was treated in the book, Mark asks the class about him.)

Mark: How about Boo Radley, class? What do you think about him?

Ruth Boedigheimer: Ruth Boedigheimer, Mr. Dowdle.

Mark: Yes, Ruth.

Ruth: I think Boo was a very lonely man. He wasn't accepted by others in the town just because he was different, and I think that's very sad.

Mark: Well, Ruth, I do, too. What are we to think about those who are unlike us?

(Nobody answers, so Mark continues speaking.)

Mark: I think Jean Louise or Scout possessed the answer. She accepted Boo Radley just the way he was, and she understood and liked him in spite of his being different. Boo felt the same way about Scout, and that's why you see him protecting her near the end of the book.

(The deep-felt class discussion continues until the bell rings. The 9th graders don't rush from the room even though it's the last class of the day. They file out slowly, still pondering all that has been talked about that hour.)

NARRATOR: Friday afternoon, the 7th graders seem a little unsettled about having to write a composition in class for their first grade in English. In grade school you are able to take the writing assignment home and get help from your parents.)

Mark: Okay, class. You know what the assignment is. I've talked about it enough! Go to work! You've got the whole hour to write! I'll collect the papers at the end of the hour and have them back to you on Monday, corrected and graded.

(You could have heard a pin drop during the whole hour, and five minutes before the bell rang, the 7th graders were sweating and out of there. It didn't take the 8th or 9th graders long to begin comparing their families to the ones in *The Diary of Anne Frank* and *To Kill a Mockingbird*. They meant business! What Mark could feel, but not see, was the intensity with which they approached the assignment. Joey Gentilli never once raised his head as he wrote.)

NARRATOR: When the bell rang, Mark was out of there. He was feeling upbeat as Prince and he headed for home, looking forward to a relaxing weekend and having Chuck read what his students had written about their families. What Mark didn't realize was that he was about to be deeply affected and have his confidence shaken by a headline in the upcoming Sunday paper.

Chuck: (shaking his head and looking down as he walks in the room, open newspaper in hand) I can't believe it!

Marty: What is it?

Chuck: (reads headline aloud as he holds the paper up for Marty and Linda to see)

PERHAM HIGH SCHOOL STUDENT COMMITS SUICIDE

(Everyone gasps audibly.)

Chuck: (somberly) School has barely started and something like this happens?

Linda: This is terrible. Does it say who it is?

Chuck: (scanning the article) It says the student is Joey Gentilli. Do you recognize the name, Mark?

(Mark feels like he's been hit with a sledgehammer. He crumples forward in his chair, bends over with his head in his hands and begins sobbing uncontrollably. Linda puts her arm around Mark's shoulder. Everyone remains silent for several minutes until Mark raises his head.)

Mark: (numbly) I have him in braille and English. Just this week, early Monday morning before class started, he came into my room and began telling me how upsetting it was for him to read about the way Boo Radley was treated in *To Kill a Mockingbird* just because he was different. I told him it was a topic worth discussing in class, which we did Friday afternoon. I gave the students a writing assignment, which was to compare the Finch family to their own. I remember Joey questioning whether that might be a bit personal. I'll go get the papers and we can see what Joey wrote.

(Mark has his dad read Joey's paper for him.)

Chuck:

Dear Mr. Dowdle,

I've enjoyed being in both your Braille and English classes this first week of school and have enjoyed talking with you. You listened to me with your heart, it seemed, and treated me with respect, and I appreciated that more than anything. I don't get much of that from students or at home from my mother or older sister. My dad died in an auto accident when I was just a kid, and I don't remember much about him.

Life has been pretty tough at school and at home for me. The kids at school and my mom and older sister have teased me about my cleft palate and lisp for as long as I can remember. Believe me, Mr. Dowdle, my life has not been anything like Scout's in "To Kill a Mockingbird." Scout's father, Atticus, loved and respected her. In a way, I envied her and wished he could have been my father.

When you and I were talking, I mentioned I thought it was unfair the way Boo Radley was treated. After the class discussion, I began thinking about how long I've been mistreated by students, my mother and sister, just as were Boo Radley and Tom Robinson, all of us simply because we're different. Tom was innocent of any wrongdoing, just like Boo, and a jury convicted him.

Mr. Dowdle, I'm tired of not being accepted by students and my mother and sister just because I'm a little different and don't fit in. Being taunted by them every day has been like living in a prison. I do not feel respected or loved. I'm ready to break out, to be free, sooner rather than later.

—*Your friend, Joey Gentilli*

Mark: (numbly) I just can't believe it. I can't believe he's gone.

NARRATOR: Monday morning during Mark's first period Braille class, the students are subdued as they take their seats and get to work. Mark hears a light knock at the door, and Mr. Pfenninger, the principal, opens it quietly and walks over to Mark's desk. He bends his head near Mark and whispers in his ear.

Mr. Pfenninger: Mr. Pfenninger, Mark. I have Joey Gentilli's mother outside in the hallway. She's come to gather Joey's things and to have a word with his teachers, if possible. Would you have time to speak with her if I sit in with your class?

(Mark reaches for his briefcase with one hand and Prince's leather handle with the other.)

Mark: Of course.

(As Mark walks out of the classroom, Mrs. Gentilli approaches him.)

Mrs. Gentilli: Thank you for taking the time to speak with me, Mr. Dowdle.

Mark: I'm so very sorry, Mrs. Gentilli. It's heartbreaking. Let's head down the hall to Mr. Pfenninger's office where we can talk in private.

> (Mr. Pfenninger sits at Mark's desk and just observes. He can't help but notice the one conspicuously empty desk, Joey Gentilli's. The second thing he notices is how industriously the Braille students go about their work, concentrating on it, eyes closed. He's impressed as he watches their fingers patiently work their way across the rows of raised-dot letters.)

Mark: (somberly after they are seated in the principal's office) Mrs. Gentilli, I was completely crushed when my father read the news to me about Joey. As you know, I had Joey for Braille and English.

Mrs. Gentilli: Sits quietly and nods, not thinking about Mark's blindness.

Mark: The only thing I have to give you is a composition I had the 9th graders write last Friday. I was going to hand them back today, and you're certainly welcome to have Joey's.

Mrs. Gentilli: That would mean a lot to me Mr. Dowdle.

Mark: (reaches into his briefcase and fingers through the contents; hands stack of sixth period compositions to Mrs.

Gentilli) Would you mind looking through these and finding Joey's for me, Mrs. Gentilli?

Mrs. Gentilli: I'd be happy to.

(Mrs. Gentilli leafs through the papers and finds her son's composition.)

Mark: I could tell from Joey's composition that he was an extremely sensitive boy, Mrs. Gentilli. It seems he was hurting, and at some level, crying for help. I think you'll see what I mean when you read what he wrote.

Mrs. Gentilli: (rises to leave) Well, Mr. Dowdle, I won't take any more of your time. Thank you very much for seeing me.

(Mark and Prince walk back to his classroom. Mr. Pfenninger gets up from the desk when Mark enters the room and whispers in his ear.)

Mr. Pfenninger: I'm really impressed with these kids. They haven't stopped working for a second. How did it go with Mrs. Gentilli?

Mark: (quietly) It was okay. I think she's in a state of shock. I gave her the composition Joey wrote last Friday. It was about some of his struggles at home. I think it will be very difficult for her and Joey's older sister to read.

Mr. Pfenninger: (puts his hands on Mark's shoulder and sighs deeply) I really appreciate you taking the time to talk with her. I know it wasn't easy.

Mark: I appreciate you giving me the opportunity. This is a rough time for all of us. Thanks again for sitting in.

(When Mark meets with his 9th grade English class, it's much like his earlier 7th and 8th grade English classes. He tells them to move the desks into groups of three or five for their next writing assignment and to sit with whichever group they'd like.)

Mark: This week I'd like you to imagine that you lived where the characters in the book you just read lived, and at that time, and that you are an adult and a writer for a newspaper. Your job is to create a newspaper with all of the different kinds of articles that go into a newspaper. You can have comics, ads, and everything else that goes into a newspaper. Sign your name for your individual work, so I'll know who gets the credit when I grade your newspaper. The paper is due on Friday. You may have the rest of the period and week to work, and feel free to refer to the books on the shelf for names of persons, places, etc. Before you get started, I'd like to ask one of you to hand back the compositions from last week. I certainly know more about you and your families now than when we first met. Thank you for sharing your thoughts and feelings with me. I know we're all feeling stunned and saddened by the news about Joey Gentilli. If he was here to share his composition with you today, you'd be able to see into his heart. You'd hear him say how unfair it was for Boo Radley and Tom Robinson to be mistreated just because they were different. Joey thought of himself as different because he had a cleft palate and spoke with a lisp, and he yearned to be accepted in spite of it. It's an important lesson for all of us, the importance of kindness. Use the rest of the time to begin working on your newspaper.

NARRATOR: The second week passes quickly, and all of Mark's English classes need more time for their newspapers, so he gives them a third week to finish. It seems like from then on it isn't a matter of days or weeks or months that pass quickly, but years!

At the beginning of Mark's second year of teaching, Linda is hired to teach History and Business Law at Perham High School. Her sister Laurie begins working as a nurse, and both women have babysitters for William Francis and Gretchen Marie. Michael is doing real well with Minneapolis Pharmaceuticals and Mark is settling into a comfortable and enjoyable teaching routine. Chuck, on the other hand, is beginning to look forward to retirement with Marty more and more. It seems, also, that teaching has become such a vital part of Mark's life, especially the writing aspect, that he has little time for anything else, even for his son, William Francis, who is now in the first grade.

It is near the end of the school year when William Francis's first grade teacher has the children write a story about the most important people in their lives. William Francis can hardly wait to get started, and when he finishes, he can hardly wait to share what he's written with his mom and dad. On the last day of school, papers in hand, he runs home and rushes into the house.

William Francis: Mom! Dad!

(Calls for his parents, but all he gets is a husky bark from Prince in the backyard, so he races outside.)

Linda (sitting and relaxing in the shade with Mark) You're looking pretty hot and sweaty, mister! You must have run all the way home!

William Francis: (breathlessly, as he hands Linda his papers and stands between his parents) I did! I did!

Linda: What's all this?

William Francis: It's my writing from this year! The most important one is right on top! I wrote it this week! Can you read it to Dad now?

Linda (takes the top paper from the pile and places the rest on the patio table next to her) What's this story about?

William Francis: Just read it, Mom, and you and Dad will find out!

Mark: I'm listening!

Linda: (reading) "*My dad is blind. He's a teacher at my school. A lot of the time when my dad is home he is busy reading papers. My grandpa helps him since he can't see. Sometimes me and my dad go out for long walks with our dog, Prince. Those are the times I like best, the times when we're together. My mom is a teacher, too. She is a really good cook! She is really nice and I like talking with her. My mom has more time to spend with me since she doesn't have all those papers to read. When I come home from school, she always asks how my day has been. My mom and dad are the most important people in my life. I love them very much, and I love Prince, too.*"

Linda: (glances over at Mark and can see his eyes tearing up) What a nice paper, William Francis! (gives William Francis a hug)

Mark: (reaches over to embrace his son) It sure is! You're a born writer!

William Francis: (sees a tear streaming down his dad's face) Are you sad, Dad?

Mark: (affectionately) That writing came straight from your heart. It was just so good that it got to me.

Linda: (emotional and smiling at her son) You must be thirsty, William Francis! How about a glass of lemonade?

William Francis: Sure!

Linda (turns her head from her son so he won't see her tears as she stands up, heads for the house and calls back over her shoulder) It's the end of the school year, time for us to celebrate!

William Francis: (talks to his dad while Linda's in the house) Maybe we can celebrate by going to visit Uncle Michael and Auntie Laurie and Gretchen! Please, Dad!

Mark: Maybe we can. I'll talk it over with your mom.

> (After supper that night, with William Francis off to bed, Linda and Mark sit down and have a long talk about what their son has written. Mark feels like an arrow has pierced his heart.)

Mark: (somberly) That little guy's words really got to me. I'm definitely going to ease up on the hours of work I do at home and spend more time with him.

Linda: That would be wonderful! He certainly treasures your time with him.

Mark: Also, while you were getting his lemonade this afternoon, he leaned into me and basically pleaded for us to visit his cousin this summer. What do you think?

Linda: (laughing) I'd love to, of course! It's been too long since we were together, and we've got lots of catching up to do. I'll call Laurie and see if there's a weekend that will work out for them.

Mark: (early the next morning at breakfast) How'd you like to go fishing this morning William Francis?

William Francis: Sure, Dad!

(William Francis is thrilled and it doesn't take long for him to gulp down his cereal, get dressed, and be waiting at the door.)

William Francis: (yelling) Ready, Dad!

Linda: (laughs) Easy there, William Francis! I'm still packing a lunch for you two.

Mark: (father and son walk hand in hand into the garage) And we have to get all our fishing gear.

NARRATOR: Linda enjoys fishing, too, but she wants the morning to be a special father/son bonding time for Mark and William Francis. Besides, a few hours to relax in the peaceful back yard sounds heavenly and will give her some time to call her sister.

After talking with Laurie, the sisters agree that Father's Day weekend would work out great for the families to gather. They will arrive on Friday and stay until Monday, with Father's Day of course being on Sunday. Marty and Chuck will come along, too, and stay with Walter and Grace.

(The first thing Linda does when Mark and William Francis return from fishing at Little Pine Lake is to tell William Francis that he'll soon be visiting his cousin.)

Linda: Well, William Francis, I talked to your Auntie Laurie. We'll soon be going to see her and Uncle Michael and Gretchen for a whole weekend. We'll be leaving on Friday and Grandma and Grandpa will come with us, too!

(William Francis jumps up and down and yells and runs off to look for his dad to tell him.)

William Francis: (yelling) Dad! Dad! Mom said we're going to see Gretchen next weekend! She just told me! And Grandma and Grandpa are coming, too!

Mark: (laughing) Whoa! That's big news! We're going to have lots of fun together!

Narrator: Gretchen is seven years old now, having just celebrated her birthday on June 7th, and it will be interesting to see how she's grown and changed. William Francis will soon follow her when he turns seven on August 8th.)

(When Chuck and Marty and Mark and Linda pull up in front of Laurie and Michael's Coon Rapids home on Friday, the first person who comes out of the house to greet them is Gretchen. She immediately runs to William Francis and gives him a big hug.)

Gretchen: (yelling) Hi, William Francis!

(William Francis quickly notices how strong Gretchen is as she holds him.)

William Francis: (somewhat shyly) Hi, Gretchen.

Chuck: Hey! What about us?

Gretchen: Hi, Grandma and Grandpa! Hi Auntie Linda! Hi Uncle Mark! (gives them all a big hug)

(Once the young cousins are in the house, it doesn't take long for them to get re-acquainted and feel at home with each other.)

Gretchen: Do you want to go outside in the front yard and play, William Francis?

(Play is always a magic word with kids, and in no time at all the cousins are outside playing a game of tag.)

Gretchen: (shouting) I'll be it!

(William Francis is light and fast, and he runs towards the sidewalk to get away from Gretchen. As they run down the sidewalk, Gretchen stumbles forward and flies flat onto her stomach, hitting her chin on the concrete.)

William Francis: (screams and runs towards the house) Mom! Dad! Come outside! Hurry! Gretchen's bleeding! She fell and hurt herself!

(Laurie is the first one out the door, with everyone else close behind. She gasps when she sees Gretchen sitting on the sidewalk, blood dripping from her chin.)

Laurie: Honey! What did you do?

Gretchen: (crying) I fell, Mommy!

Laurie: Let's get you into the house and fix up that chin!

(William Francis runs to Linda and sees tears in her eyes.)

William Francis: Mom, I didn't do anything! Gretchen was just chasing me and she fell!

Linda: I know, darling. Don't worry, she'll be all right. But no more tag, okay?

William Francis: (somberly) Okay.

(Michael, Mark, Marty and Chuck walk over to the sidewalk and are examining it. Michael sees the part of the walk that is cracked and lifted up a couple of inches from the ground.)

Michael: This must be the place where she tripped. It's going to get fixed, that's for sure!

(When Walter and Grace arrive, Gretchen's chin has stopped bleeding and she has a bandage on it.)

Walter: What happened to you, young lady?

Gretchen: I fell on the sidewalk, Grandpa.

(Grace and Walter listen carefully as Laurie fills them in on all the details.)

Grace: (reaches down to Gretchen and gives her a hug and kisses the top of her head) It'll get better, honey. Remember, your mom's a nurse, and she knows how to fix up little girls when they fall.

Gretchen: I know Granny.

(There is a lot of talk, and it is already six o'clock and nobody has mentioned anything about food.)

Laurie: Oh my! It's late! Everyone must be starving! So much has been happening, I haven't even thought about eating! Everything is pretty much ready. I just have to warm up a couple of things in the oven.

Grace: (cheerfully, as she follows her daughter into the kitchen with Marty and Linda) We'll help you!

Laurie: (opens the refrigerator and begins handing things out) Okay, Mom, why don't you set the table, and Marty, you can help with that if you don't mind. Linda and I will get the food ready.

Marty: Of course!

Grace: (laughing) C'mon, Marty. We can handle this. Plus, it'll give us a chance to catch up.

NARRATOR: Preparing the food gives Linda and Laurie a chance to do the same, and they take advantage of it. They talk about school and how the kids are doing in first grade. Linda begins telling Laurie about the paper William Francis wrote about the important people in his life.

Linda: It was really insightful, and Mark and I were pretty taken aback by what he said.

Laurie: What did he say that surprised you?

Linda: (sighs) Well, he basically said his dad was blind and was a teacher and was always busy with Grandpa reading papers and that neither of them had much time to spend with him. We thought it was pretty sad when we read it, but it's true.

Laurie: Wow! I'll bet Mark and you had a long talk after that revelation!

Linda: We sure did. William Francis wrote that he liked how I talk with him and take the time to ask how his day has gone. Can you believe that, Laurie? He said I was a teacher and a good cook, too, but the one thing he most valued from Mark and me was our time.

Laurie: Boy, what did you two decide to do?

Linda: What else? To make time for him and to learn to listen!

Laurie: That's good advice for every parent. Michael and I have certainly learned to do that with Gretchen.

Linda: I'll bet you have. Tell me a little about her.

Laurie: Well, like other babies born with Down syndrome, she'll have more medical and learning challenges than other children, but she's all love and wants to be a nurse like me. That will never happen, of course, but she has an indomitable spirit. Gretchen is very friendly, and she has taught Michael and me so much about the real value of life. I could talk for hours about that, but let's get the food on the table or we'll be in trouble!

(Grace and Marty have finished setting the table and they join Laurie and Linda in delivering ham that has been warmed in the oven, a crock of Boston baked beans, a large bowl of potato salad, and a basket of hot buns and fresh butter. They don't have to call the men and William Francis to the table. As soon as the aromas fill the air, Mark is on his feet with Prince and they lead everyone else to the dining room.)

Walter: (enthusiastically as they all take their seats) Wow! This is quite a feast!

Laurie: I had planned on making dessert, too, but with everything happening today, I just didn't have time.

Grace: You don't have to worry, honey. I brought dessert. It's still in the car.

Gretchen: What did you bring, Granny?

Grace: You'll have to wait, Gretchen. It's a surprise! Now it's time to pray.

Michael: *Lord, please bless this family, and especially Gretchen, who took quite a tumble out there on the sidewalk this afternoon. Please help her chin to heal. And thank you for this delicious food Laurie and Linda prepared, Lord. Amen.*

Everyone: *Amen!*

Walter: (looks lovingly at his daughter) This ham is wonderful, Laurie! I sure like the way you prepare it!

Laurie: Thanks, Dad, but the honors go to Mom. I fix it the same way she does, just like everything else I make.

(Everyone laughs and keeps right on eating.)

Gretchen: Just about time for dessert, Granny. What did you bring?

Grace: I'll let your dad go and get it. It's outside in the trunk of the car.

(Michael takes the car keys from Grace and goes outside. He comes back carrying a magnificent pineapple upside-down cake!)

Everyone: Wow!

Grace: I made it special for all of you.

Gretchen: Yum! Thank you, Granny! I can hardly wait! It's one of my favorite desserts!

(By the time everyone polishes off a piece of Grace's delicious pineapple upside-down cake, it's starting to get dark outside and everyone is beginning to feel the fatigue of a long day.)

Walter: I think we'd better be heading home.

Chuck: I agree, Walter. Marty and I will get our things and be right with you.

(It has been a long and emotional day, and after the grandparents say their goodbyes, everyone heads off to bed for a good night's sleep.)

Laurie: (big sigh) I hope Gretchen's doing okay!

Michael: Of course she is, sweetheart. You fixed her chin, and the main thing she was interested in tonight was Granny's dessert. Try to get some sleep.

(Seconds later, Michael is breathing heavily and fast asleep. Laurie can't help but smile as she looks lovingly at her husband.)

Laurie: (says quietly to herself) How do men do it?

(Even though she sleeps fitfully, Laurie is the first one up in the morning, and by the time the others have awakened, she has breakfast on the table. Surprisingly, Gretchen and William Francis are the next ones up. Laurie kisses her daughter on the forehead.)

Laurie: Oh, honey, it's so good to see you up and smiling! How do you feel?

Gretchen: My chin hurts a little, but it's not bad.

William Francis: I'm sorry for making you fall, Gretchen.

Gretchen: It wasn't your fault, William Francis. It was that dumb sidewalk!

(Laurie smiles when she hears Gretchen say that because the nurse in her knows that her daughter is on her way to a full recovery. After breakfast, Gretchen seems happy to just curl up on the sofa and rest quietly. Prince senses that she's been hurt and settles in by her side as she pets him tenderly. Then the phone rings.)

Laurie: Hi, Mom.

Grace: (enthusiastically) Hi, sweetheart! There was so much commotion yesterday that I forgot to tell you before we left that we want all of you to come to our house for supper tomorrow for Father's Day! Tell Gretchen I'm going to make her favorite dessert, angel food cake with pink frosting!

Laurie: She'll be happy about that! It all sounds wonderful, Mom. Thanks for the invitation!

Grace: How is my little granddaughter doing after her fall?

Laurie: She just ate breakfast and seems to be doing just fine, Mom. She's sitting on the sofa and resting now, but she seems to be over her fall. Her only complaint is that her chin is a little sore.

Grace: That's great, Laurie! I won't take any more of your time. We'll count on seeing all of you tomorrow for supper. Just come any time in the late afternoon.

Laurie: Okay, Mom. We'll see you tomorrow. Thanks for calling!

(A peaceful Saturday morning gives the young couples an opportunity to get all caught up.)

Laurie: I can't believe it. We had such grandiose ideas when we left college, got married and started grad school. That just goes to show how the best laid plans don't always pan out.

Linda: (laughing) That's for sure, but it seems we're all happy, so kudos to us!

Mark: (leans over and kisses his wife) I know I am! I never thought of myself as a teacher, but the job has been totally satisfying and rewarding. I don't know what life might have been like as an attorney, but I'm guessing somewhat boring compared to what I'm doing now, so I'm just going to enjoy every day of being with my students for as long as I can.

Linda: I feel the same way about teaching that Mark does. We won't be getting rich any- time soon, but it really is enjoyable work. How about you, Laurie?

Laurie: (laughs) We're in way over our heads in keeping up with our lives! All you have to do is look around our house to see we're living in a zoo! It's going to be a long time before I have a chance to practice my nursing full time.

Michael: (laughing) Outside of the house, at least! Gretchen has a vision problem, but she likes to run and does a lot of falling.

Laurie: That's for sure! I definitely have my hands full. But we love being parents and Michael makes a good living for us, so it's all working out.

Linda: I can see how happy you are, Laurie. How's your work going, Michael?

Michael: Well, my company has been having me spend more time in the lab. There are a lot of exciting studies being financed and new machines being developed. In a way, I'm not disappointed that I wasn't able to become a doctor. I've always been intrigued by research that leads to new discoveries, and that's exactly what my company is allowing me to focus on.

NARRATOR: Everyone sleeps in on Sunday morning, even Laurie, and by the time they've eaten breakfast and gotten home from eleven o'clock Mass at Church of the Epiphany in Coon Rapids, there is time for the adults to visit before heading to Grace and Walter's house for supper.

After they arrive at Grace and Walter's house, the talk is all about kids, grandkids and retirement.

Chuck: I plan to put in a few more years and then call it quits. I love teaching English, but with all the papers to read, I think I spend as many hours working on class-related things at home as I do at school. I'll stick it out for another six years and then start enjoying retirement.

Grace: That'd be 1988, Chuck. Is there a particular reason you picked that year?

Chuck: Not really, other than that I will have turned 60 and am getting tired of correcting all the writing assignments. Don't get me wrong, I love communicating with my students by reading what's in their heads and hearts and giving them feedback, but I'm not going to miss hauling home a stack of papers every week.

Walter: How do you feel about Chuck retiring, Marty?

Marty: I'm fine with it. I'll be especially fine with it when I can come home from work and dinner's waiting!

Walter: (grinning broadly as Chuck smiles) Did you hear that, Chuck?

Chuck: (smiling) Hear what?

Marty: It's hard to believe I've been working just as long as Chuck. No papers to correct, but being a physical therapist takes its toll. I'm sure I'll be ready to retire along with Chuck when the time comes.

Chuck: How about you, Walter?

Walter: To tell you the truth, I haven't given it much thought, even though I know it's time to start doing so. We aren't getting any younger, and it would be nice to do some traveling and other things Grace and I have talked about.

Grace: I think you've been consumed by your building work the same way Chuck has been by his dedication to his students and Marty to her patients. It's been a lot of years of your lives, and you'll no doubt miss it very much.

Marty: I know you're right, Grace.

Chuck: Unfortunately, I think maybe we've all been living too much for our work.

Walter: I don't know about that. I love my work! I don't see anything wrong with that. You have to have money to buy a home and eat and take care of your children, and the only way to make money is to work.

Chuck: True enough, Walter, it's just that there are things in life that are equally important, especially when you're raising a family! Linda and Mark were reminded of that recently when William Francis brought home some heartfelt thoughts he'd written at school about the most important people in his life. He said his dad was blind and didn't have much time to spend with him because he was always correcting papers. He said his mom worked, too, and that she was a great cook, but what he liked most was when she took time to sit with him and talk. That was what he most treasured, being able to share time with his mom and dad.

Grace: I'll bet that was an eye opener for Linda and Mark.

Marty: More than you can imagine! Linda was glad to learn William Francis liked her cooking, but she most valued his expressing how much he liked talking with her. Now Mark and Linda are making a special effort to spend more time with William Francis.

Grace: That's very interesting. It seems Michael has been heavily involved in his work, too, and Laurie, of course, has been one busy woman from the day Gretchen was born. I've never heard Gretchen say anything about wanting to spend more time with her. Gretchen's usually pretending she's a nurse like her mom or playing with her little friends when she's not at school. Oh, speaking of Gretchen, there's an angel food cake in the kitchen that's waiting for some pink frosting. I thought I'd surprise her since it's her favorite dessert.

Marty: (cheerfully) That's very thoughtful of you, Grace! Let me help!

Grace: (heading out of the room) Thanks, Marty! How about you start on the frosting while I work on supper?

Marty: Sure.

(Time flies when families are having fun, especially families that love one another. Grace and Marty can be heard chatting and laughing as they work in the kitchen. Walter and Chuck are contentedly engaged in conversation in the living room. The minutes roll by, and when the front doorbell rings, they all know their peaceful afternoon is over!)

Laurie and Linda: (chorus when Walter opens the door) Happy Father's Day, Dad!

Walter: (happily) Thank you, girls! Thank you very much! And Happy Father's Day to you boys as well!

(Walter embraces his daughters and Mark and Michael.)

Walter: Come in! Come in! We can relax and visit in the living room until dinner's ready.

(It doesn't take long, and soon everyone is seated at the large dining room table.)

Michael: (enthusiastically) Everything sure looks scrumptious, Grace!

Grace: (Grace and Marty exchange smiles) Well, I couldn't have done it without Marty's help. I hope everyone likes it! Roast beef has always been one of Walter's favorite Sunday meals, as we all know, and I thought I'd better please him with it today since it's Father's Day!

Walter: (enthusiastically as he looks lovingly at his wife.) And I sure do appreciate it! Let's pray so we can get down to eating!

Father in heaven, thank You for this beautiful meal we're about to enjoy and for the two beautiful women who prepared it for us. Amen.

Laurie: (laughing) Wow! That was pretty short for you, Dad! You must be hungry!

Walter: (forking up several slices of tender beef from the platter) I am! I am! Let's eat now and talk later, like our little patient.

(Gretchen squirms in her chair and looks down, fork in hand. She is typically more reserved around all the grownups and is never one to seek the limelight.)

Laurie: Gretchen's been a perfect patient. When she grows up she wants to be a nurse just like her mother. Isn't that right, Gretchen?

(Everyone looks at Gretchen, who looks around the table until her eyes meet Laurie's.)

Gretchen: (softly) "I love you, Mommy."

(No one says anything for a few moments as they let those words sink in.)

Laurie: (warmly) "I love you, too, honey."

Grace: (after everyone has had their fill and the dishes are cleared from the table) "Anybody ready for dessert?

Gretchen: I am, Granny! Did you make a pineapple upside-down cake?

Grace: (smiles at her granddaughter) Not this time, Gretchen, but I don't think you'll be disappointed.

(Gretchen is curious and watches her granny go back into the kitchen. She soon comes out carrying a large angel food cake with pink frosting. Gretchen knows the cake is made for her because it's her favorite. Her eyes widen with delight as Grace sets the cake in front of her.)

Gretchen: Wow!

Grace: (hands Walter a knife) Your Grandpa can help with the slicing.

Walter: (winks at his granddaughter) Well, I think I know someone who's going to enjoy this!

(Gretchen doesn't say a word, just smiles as she looks up at her grandpa.)

Walter: (places a generous piece of cake on Gretchen's plate) Here you go! Let's see if you can finish that!

(Gretchen doesn't disappoint her grandpa. She keeps right up with the adults and eats every crumb.)

Gretchen: (putting down her fork) Thank you, Granny! That was so good!

(After dessert, everyone moves to the living room for some relaxing conversation. They talk about what a wonderful weekend it's been in spite of Gretchen's mishap.)

Walter: What time do Marty and you want to head out of here tomorrow, Chuck? Grace and I will drive you to Laurie and Michael's whenever you'd like.

Chuck: We'll need to leave soon after breakfast. We really want to thank you for the wonderful days we've been able to spend here with you.

Marty: We sure do. It's been so enjoyable and we really appreciate it.

Narrator: It doesn't take long the next morning for the Dowdles to regroup at Laurie and Michael's house. Grace, Walter, Marty and Chuck are up and dressed by six, done with breakfast by seven, and at Laurie and Michael's house by eight. Everyone is saying their goodbyes when they notice Gretchen and William Francis talking near the front door.)

William Francis: (quietly, as his eyes well up with tears) I'm sure glad you're feeling better, Gretchen.

Gretchen: Oh, it was nothing, just a little scratch on my chin.

NARRATOR: It's pretty obvious that William Francis is a sensitive little boy and Gretchen is a courageous little girl. It's also obvious that the two cousins like one another.

Tuesday morning after breakfast, before Marty leaves for work at the hospital, Chuck takes out some of the old student compositions he has saved so he can read them alone. William Francis finishes his bowl of oatmeal, gets up, moves to his dad's side and slides his hand into Mark's.

William Francis: Dad, I want to be a teacher.

Mark: (very touched to hear his young son say that, but doesn't know quite how to respond) Well, where did that come from?

William Francis: Gretchen says she wants to be a nurse just like her mom, and I want to be a teacher, just like you.

> (Mark sits quietly for a moment and thinks about what William Francis has written about him, about how he never seems to have time to talk with him because he is always busy correcting papers.)

Mark: (smiling) Well, William Francis, I know you will be a wonderful teacher.

William Francis: Thanks, Dad. I want to teach braille just like you. Will you teach me braille this summer?

(This kid is serious, but then so is Gretchen about becoming a nurse, and there is no way Mark is going to pass up this golden opportunity to connect with his son.)

Mark: I'll be happy to do that, and we can start right now.

(Mark can't see his son's face, but it is filled with radiant joy and anticipation.)

NARRATOR: The summer flies by, and the years begin flying by as well. When the end of the 1987-88 school year arrives, it makes Chuck a bit melancholy knowing he won't be coming back to teach, but joyful just the same! He receives many touching send-offs from his students, including these words written in his yearbook:

"Dear Mr. Dowdle,

Another year has come and gone. Incredible, isn't it? It was a wonderful year, full of exciting books to read, essays to write (yes, I did enjoy them), and topics to be debated. One of the only times I've looked forward to an argument was in your class! In our debates, you always found a way to prove me wrong, but, for some reason, that just made me feel more firmly that I was right! Your arguments taught me that with most issues, one must take a stand in order to have his/her opinion heard. You have always taken a stand on the issues over which we debated, and this in itself made the issues seem much more important.

All around, you made English a class I looked forward to every day. Thank you! Have a wonderful summer and a relaxing retirement. I consider myself really lucky to have been your student and friend."

—Leah Mundell

May 28, 1988 is a memorable day, a day of total liberation from work for Marty and Chuck. No more school and no more hospital. Will they miss it? You bet! But it is pretty nice knowing they have the freedom to do whatever they want whenever they want. All the relatives arrive on Saturday for a retirement celebration. Walter and Grace drive up from Coon Rapids early in the morning. Laurie, Michael and Gretchen arrive a bit later, and Chuck's older brother, Bill, and his family drive up from Columbia Heights, arriving in Perham around noon, just in time for lunch. It is a great time in life for the retirees, and it is a festive afternoon of high spirits, bountiful food and lively conversation. Little does Chuck realize that his brother Bill won't be with him much longer.

Bill dies of cancer a year later on June 23, 1989. Chuck asks the priest if he can give a eulogy at the funeral Mass, and the priest says it would be fine. He suggests that Chuck write out his words, as he knows people get very emotional at funerals and often forget what they want to say. Chuck takes his advice, types it up on an old manual typewriter in the basement of Bill and Pearl's house the day before the funeral, and is glad he did. The large Colombia Heights church is filled to capacity, and Chuck gets choked up when he begins speaking about his brother.

Chuck: My name is Chuck Dowdle. I'd like to say a few words about the brother I admired and loved, and who will always be with me. I can already hear Bill saying, "Charlie, Charlie, let's not go overboard now.

First, let me give you a little family background. We're from Crookston. Bill was the eldest of five children. I was second, and our sister, Betty, was third. Our sister, Cathy, who died at an early age of Parkinson's disease, was fourth, and our brother, Jerry, was the youngest. Our dad died of a heart attack and our mother is still living. Bill was a lot like Dad. He loved life, he enjoyed a good time and he loved people! When he was in the hospital, he said, "I sure wish I could go quickly like Dad did."

I got to know my brother real well when we were growing up. We shared a bedroom for about fifteen years. We shared brotherly secrets and experiences. We shared a paper route and delivered during sun, rain and freezing blizzards during the early hours of the morning. When Bill was a senior at Cathedral High School and I was a freshman going to my first school dance, I didn't know how to dance, so Bill taught me the fox trot, albeit reluctantly. It seemed that Bill was always looking out for me in a sensitive and nurturing way.

He taught me how to fish the river and he introduced me to sports, which he loved, especially baseball and ice hockey. He was catcher for the hometown American Legion baseball team and captained his high school ice hockey team. We used to go outside in the winter with Mom's pillows stuffed in our pants and take turns shooting pucks at one another. Bill even played football when he was a senior. He played end. Can you imagine a 5'7" 120 pound end?

For a short time after graduation from high school, Bill worked for the Great Northern Railroad as a fireman on a passenger train from Grand Forks to Seattle. He hated it, and that's when he decided to come to Minneapolis and look for a job. I remember seeing him off at the Greyhound Bus station. I had saved up some silver dollars to give him as a going away present. When he left, it was like a part of me left, too. Bill got a job at the Minneapolis Honeywell Regulator Company and he worked there for 42 years. He retired at 62 and died two years later at 64.

I'd like to tell you how Bill died, because I think he lived like he died, filled with courage, faith and love.

Pearl, his wife, said, "On Monday of last week, the doctor was going to come into Bill's hospital room and tell the family the results of some tests, and Bill wanted the whole family to be there. I think Bill knew what the results were going to be, because after everyone was in the room, he said, "Close the door, honey. We don't know what the doctor's going to tell us, how much time I have left, but I want to spend it with my wonderful family, and I want to tell them all how much I love them, including the sons-in-law and the grandchildren. And I want to tell them to love everybody and to love their spouses as much as I love you." Pearl said everybody began crying and telling him how much they loved him when he said that, and Bill said, "That's all right. It's good to cry. Now lighten up!"

My wife, Marty, and I entered Bill's room for the first time last Thursday morning, just as a cancer specialist was beginning to explain to Bill that his chances of surviving were extremely slim. Bill took the news fearlessly and calmly. My wife and I visited with Bill and Pearl all that day, and my brother and I got to talk about all the good times we had together, and I got to tell him how much I loved him.

Pearl, who'd been sleeping by Bill's side since he entered the hospital, called us early Friday morning and said Bill's blood pressure and pulse had dropped. The whole family got there before Bill gave up his life at around 11:00 a.m. It seemed like he was just struggling to wait until they all arrived. As he repeatedly made the sign of the cross, his dying words were: "Can't take it anymore! Bye, bye! I love you!" And then Bill stared at the ceiling as if seeing a vision, and died!

I'd like to close by speaking directly to my brother. You folks can listen in. "Don't worry about Pearl and the kids, Bill. They're following right in your footsteps. You'd be proud of them. After you died on Friday, the whole family went to Hillside Cemetery and purchased two lots, one for you and one for Pearl, right next to Pearl's mom and dad whom you loved so much. I remember how you fell in love with the whole Carlson family when you met Pearl. You put faith in Pearl and the kids to carry out your well-laid plans, Bill, and they're doing your bidding to a 'T'. Bill, you taught me what it means to be a man when you lay dying and asked God's forgiveness for any hurt you may have caused anyone. Not to worry, Brother. You were too gentle, kind, sensitive and thoughtful to hurt people. Father Jim Studer, the priest who gave you the blessing of the sick and dying, said never in his life had he seen a greater demonstration of faith in a dying man. You're home free, Brother!

Lastly, Bill, let's talk a little about love. Do you remember when you wanted to go on a double date with me because you'd met this real neat gal from Columbia Heights? You wanted me to check her out. I didn't know whom to go with, and you said, "How about that Kirkwood girl you went to high school with? She lives in Minneapolis." Those two gals became our wives. We sure knew how to pick them, Brother!

Bill, it has to be true that home is where the heart is, because the love your family is showing for one another right now is extremely touching. I think you taught us all a good lesson about how to go about understanding and caring for people. Your whole family seems to have developed your touch, Bill. They love one another!

I think you knew all along you were going, Bill. You just waited so all of us could be here with you. Your spirit lives, Brother. Thank you for showing us the way. We love you!"

NARRATOR: On the drive back to Perham, Chuck and Marty reminisce about how their own parents had passed away, and talk about how fragile life is and how they intend to spend whatever time they have left.

Marty: The past year has been relaxing, and the traveling we've done to Washington, D.C. and Canada was fun, but now I want to begin something more regular, something to help other people.

Chuck: What do you have in mind?

Marty: I'd like to volunteer someplace where they really need me.

Chuck: (glances over at his wife and smiles) I know just where that place is!

Marty: Where?

Chuck: The hospital, of course! Where else? You know they can always use extra help, and no doubt they'd love to have you back!

Marty: Well, maybe so. I'll go over there tomorrow and see what they say.

> (What they say when she walks through the hospital doors is how much they miss her, and when she tells them she is thinking of volunteering a couple of days a week, they embrace the possibility of her return with open-armed enthusiasm.)

NARRATOR: Life moves right along for the Dowdles until the year 2000. That's when major changes begin taking place. The most challenging one occurs shortly after Chuck and Marty's 49th wedding anniversary on June 9th.

Marty: It keeps feeling like I have rocks in my stomach.

Chuck: (concerned) Honey, I think you should see a doctor.

Marty: I think it'll go away. I'll give it a little more time.

NARRATOR: It doesn't go away, and when Marty finally does see a doctor on July 19th, she is diagnosed with Stage IV ovarian cancer. Marty dies just four weeks later. Needless to say, it is devastating for Chuck and all the family. He sits down and writes these words about his beautiful wife ☺:

"Marilyn Dowdle"

Chuck: On Sunday, August 20, 2000 at 11:40 a.m., the love of my life, my wife, Marilyn "Marty" Kirkwood Dowdle, my buddy and best friend, died of ovarian cancer. As she took her last soft breaths, I held her hand and told her how much I loved her. She died peacefully, with no pain, no nausea, and a smile on her face.

Earlier that same morning, she'd been going through hell! She was receiving Demerol via a computerized pump, and I was pumping an extra shot into her body every ten minutes. It wasn't enough to handle the breakthrough pain. When my daughter-in-law, Linda, came in, she immediately called Home Hospice, and Patty Shribbs, an angel as far as I'm concerned, came to the house. She asked if I wanted Marty to have suppositories to relieve the pain. I said, "Yes!" as I certainly didn't want her to be suffering. Patty gave her two Nembutal suppositories and the pain subsided. It was a bittersweet moment for me, relieved as I was to have my wife free of pain and nausea, and at the same time feeling the sadness of impending loss.

That evening I put on one of our favorite songs, "All the Way" sung by Frank Sinatra, and I started dancing around the living room, as if I was holding Marty in my arms. I soon began hyperventilating and crying uncontrollably, and it feels like I haven't stopped since. For those of you who've been there, you know what I mean. Why, I'm crying like a baby as I sit and write this, but I don't care. I want all my tears to flow out naturally for the person I loved more than anyone else in my life.

My two sons run a close second in the love department. I don't know what I would have done without Mark and Michael. The day after their mom was told she had cancer, Michael arrived early the next morning from Coon Rapids to be with her, and Mark and he sat on either side of their mom, Mark with his head pressed gently against hers, and Michael holding her hand while they talked.

Michael drove us to Minneapolis to consult with a surgical oncologist, who informed Marty that she basically had three options: 1) Do nothing; 2) Inject the liver, which was already three times its normal size; 3) Have surgery. Marty prayed about it all that night and opted for surgery. We were all feeling a level of relief, cautiously optimistic that the surgery would be successful and that she'd be on her way to recovery. Sadly, that's not the way it happened.

After a week in the hospital in Minneapolis, where my sons and I took turns spending days and nights in her room, we were finally able to bring her home to Perham. She had a Fentanyl patch for pain and Compazine for nausea, but as it turned out, neither was adequate. Fortunately, Michael's wife, Laurie, took time off from work and arrived in time to help out.

Needless to say, it was the most difficult week of our lives. Marty was experiencing a great deal of incisional leakage and breakthrough pain, and it was gut wrenching for all of us to witness her tearful pleas for it to just be over. "All I want to do is die! Just help me die!" were her cries, but there was little we could do beyond staying at her side and praying for the pain medication to take effect. Believe me, if Marty had had the necessary medicine within reach to end her life, I would have helped her. She and I shared a belief in the right to die without unnecessary pain when one is terminally ill, which she obviously was. The doctor had given her a prognosis of less than six months.

Marty lived just three weeks after surgery, four weeks from the time of her diagnosis. Difficult as those four weeks were, they weren't completely devoid of smiles. One of the two drugs she was taking caused her to hallucinate. She said she heard Tex Beneke playing and saw Spanish dancers. We both chuckled over that. She also had a good laugh when I came home with my head shaved right before she went into surgery. I figured if she was going to undergo chemotherapy and end up losing all her hair, I wanted to be right there with her. She wasn't exactly thrilled with the look. I think her comment was, "Oh, no!" My bald head did provide us all with some much-needed comic relief over the days to come.

Marty could have opted for chemotherapy after her surgery, but having been told by the surgeon postoperatively that the cancer was incurable, she chose not to do so. She was already weak from the surgery and could actually tolerate pain more than nausea, so she was firm in her decision to forego chemotherapy. After being at home for a week post-surgery, Marty was re-admitted to the hospital for care for her incision and pain stabilization. While she was there, Mark and Linda and Laurie took turns relieving me so I could check on things at home and try to get a few hours of sleep.

I sing the praises of my wife! She was a fortress of courage. I sing the praises of all women! They're the saints of this world as far as I'm concerned. I know my wife was. She put everyone before herself, always. She was the inveterate volunteer, and was always gently suggesting that it would be good for me to give it a try. Now, I think I will.

So, there you have it, surgery in Minneapolis the first week, all hell breaking loose the second week, back in the hospital the third week, and discharged to home on Hospice Care the last week.

Let me tell you a little about the fourth and final week with Marty. Many beautiful moments were shared in the midst of the pain and sadness. Her sons were able to have intimate talks with their mom, talks that were life changing for them. "Don't sweat the small stuff, boys," she told them. "You both look so sad! I just want to hug the two of you every time I see you."

Marty was thankful she had the opportunity to say goodbye to each of us in this way, and so were we. We will treasure those moments until the day we die.

(We all celebrated the way we sent Marty off, the way she wanted it, no newspaper notice, no funeral, just her ashes spread at the rose garden near the cemetery.)

Chuck: (thinking) I honored your request, honey! I love you and always will!

NARRATOR: Marty's passing was not the last of a death spiral that was about to take place in the family. Walter and Grace hadn't attended the funeral, as they'd been experiencing their own health problems. Walter had suffered a heart attack and was confined to the house while Grace looked after him. Sadly, they were soon both gone. Walter died of a second heart attack on November 19th and Grace died the following month on December 18th.

The holidays were a difficult and mournful time for all the Dowdles, especially so for Laurie and Linda. Chuck was the only one left of the old guard, and he did his best to comfort his daughters-in-law and grandkids. At the same time, he didn't quite know what to do. The house was hollow and lonely without Marty. It felt empty, as did his heart.

After several weeks of feeling lost, Chuck decided to get away, to get into a happier environment for a while. He decided he'd take a flight to California, rent a car, and head south down the coast, rekindling relationships with friends and relatives along the way. And he did just that! His first stop was in Cambria, California for a visit with Carmelle Johnson Matthes, an old high school friend whose husband of 50 years had recently passed away.

Carmelle had been a close friend of Marty's, and Chuck had been in the same grade with the two of them at Cathedral High School in Crookston, Minnesota. He never really got close to either until after being discharged from the Navy on Thanksgiving Day in 1947. He asked Carmelle out to a New Year's Eve dance at the Crookston Armory. They danced the night away and then walked home hand-in-hand through the snow, cuddling in the warmth of a large cozy sofa once they reached Carmelle's home. It was a memorable date for Chuck, and now here he was, meeting up with Carmelle again, and as it turns out, just as smitten by her charm as he had been decades ago. To say he was riding high on a cloud when he continued south the next day barely touches the towering tip of the joy he was feeling, especially after so many weeks of utter grief and despair.

The next stop on his California journey took him to Tustin, California, where he visited with an old teaching friend and his spouse. The first thing Bill Wegner's wife, Marge, said to Chuck when they sat down to talk was that there was something different about him. As Marge told him, "I can't quite put my finger on it, Chuck, but there's definitely something different about you."

Boy, was she right! Chuck was in love! His last California stop before heading home was in San Diego to see his cousin, Bill Carter. Bill's wife had passed away, and he was alone, too. When Chuck told him he'd stopped to visit the former Carmelle Johnson in Cambria, Bill said, "It's pretty obvious you have strong feelings for her, Charlie," and he was right.

After Chuck left his cousin's house and began driving back to San Francisco, he thought about stopping to see Carmelle again before flying home to Minnesota, but he thought the better of it and begrudgingly passed on by. Instead, he wrote to her when he got back to Perham, and she wrote back to him, and after many more such exchanges, they developed a loving distance relationship. Carmelle eventually flew to Minnesota to visit him, and that clinched it! They were married on April 21st, 2001. Chuck sold his house and moved to Cambria, California, and he never looked back. That's what love will do!

Chuck wanted Mark and Michael to appreciate firsthand how their dad's life had changed over the years, and he and Carmelle decided to fly their two families out to California for Carmelle's and his 15th wedding anniversary on April 21st, 2016. Everyone was invited, and wonderfully enough, all were able to make it, even Gretchen, who was now 41 years old.

They all arrived at the San Luis Obispo Airport the day before the celebration. Chuck and Carmelle picked them up in a large rented van. The first stop was the Cambria Pines Lodge where Chuck had arranged for them to stay. It was very convenient, located right across the street from Chuck and Carmelle's house.

After a good night's sleep and a hearty breakfast at the lodge, Chuck and Carmelle picked them all up in the van and they drove to Santa Rosa Catholic Church in time to say the Rosary, which was followed by 9:00 a.m. Mass. William Francis, who'd yet to marry, sat with his parents, Mark and Linda, and Gretchen sat with Michael and Laurie.

After the Rosary and Mass, Father Mark Stetz, the pastor, asked everyone to remain seated and announced that Carmelle and Chuck were going to renew their wedding vows. He motioned for Carmelle and Chuck to approach the altar, and when they stood in front of him, he began to speak.

Father Mark Stetz: Please join your right hands and repeat after me. "*I, Charles Dowdle, take you, Carmelle Dowdle, to be my wife.*"

Chuck: I, Charles Dowdle, take you, Carmelle Dowdle, to be my wife.

Father Mark: "*I promise to be true to you, in good times and in bad, in sickness and in health.*"

Chuck: I promise to be true to you, in good times and in bad, in sickness and in health.

Father Mark: "*I will love you and honor you all the days of my life.*"

Chuck: I will love you and honor you all the days of my life.

Father Mark: (turns and smiles at Carmelle when Chuck finishes) Your turn. "*I, Carmelle Dowdle, take you, Charles Dowdle, to be my husband.*"

Carmelle: I, Carmelle Dowdle, take you, Charles Dowdle, to be my husband.

Father Mark: "*I promise to be true to you in good times and in bad, in sickness and in health.*"

Carmelle: I promise to be true to you in good times and in bad, in sickness and in health.

Father Mark: "*I will love you and honor you all the days of my life.*"

Carmelle: I will love you and honor you all the days of my life.

(At this point you could have heard a pin drop in the church.)

Father Mark: (turns to Chuck) Chuck, here before God, do you take Carmelle to be your wife?

Chuck: (answers loud and clear) I do!

Father Mark: And you, Carmelle, here before God, do you take Chuck to be your husband?

Carmelle: (answers brightly) I do!

Father Mark: (faces the twosome) "*You have declared your consent before the Church. May the Lord in His goodness strengthen your consent and fill you both with His blessings. What God has joined, men must not divide. Amen.*" Chuck, you may now kiss your beautiful bride!

(Everyone applauds as Chuck and Carmelle kiss and embrace each other warmly.)

Mark: (as Linda and he walk alongside Carmelle and Chuck on their way out of the church) That was something, Dad! It was so moving to hear Carmelle and you recommit to each other like that. Hearing those vows made me think about what it must have been like when Mom and you got married.

Chuck: It was sort of the same, but different, of course. We were so young, but there was a Mass, just like today, and your mother was beautiful, just like my lovely bride is today.

Mark: Well, I just want to say I'm very happy for both of you. You're a lucky man, Dad. Thank you both for your generosity in enabling us to be here. Linda and William Francis and I appreciate it very much.

Michael: As do Laurie and Gretchen and I! I'm so glad we were all able to be here. Thank you, Dad! And you, too, Carmelle!

Carmelle: Well, thank you everyone!

Chuck: Yes, thank you for coming! We'll see if we can continue making it worth your while for the rest of your time here. Let's pile into the van! Our next stop is the ocean and the Fiscalini Ranch Preserve boardwalk.

> (The families had never experienced the ocean, lots of lakes in Minnesota, of course, but no ocean. As they neared the ocean and could hear its roar, Gretchen got real excited.)

Gretchen: (squeals when the van pulls into full view of the ocean) That's the biggest lake I've ever seen!

Mark: (walking along slowly with Chuck on the boardwalk) This is really neat, Dad. The air smells so fresh and I love the warm breeze against my face.

> (After an anniversary dinner in the Fireplace Room at the Cambria Pines Lodge, everyone heads for their rooms for a good night's sleep because the next day is the final day

of their stay, and it is going to be a busy one. Chuck and Carmelle pick them all up after breakfast, and their first stop is the Hearst Castle. Then they travel north a few miles to view the elephant seals, which are huge and noisy.)

Gretchen: They don't look like elephants! Why do they call them elephants?

Laurie: I guess because they're so big, Gretchen, and because some of them have such big noses.

Gretchen: (smiling) Oh.

(The day's adventures end by walking along Main Street and shopping at some of Cambria's quaint, artsy stores. By late afternoon everyone is tired and ready to call it a day. Carmelle prepares a delicious salmon dinner, and Michael is the first to dig into his large filet.)

Michael: This is really good, Carmelle! I think it's the best salmon I've ever had!

Mark: And the broccoli's good, too! It tastes like it's fresh from the garden!

Carmelle: Well, thank you! I'm glad you like it.

Chuck: The cranberries are extraordinary, honey! Just had to get my two cents in.

Carmelle (laughing) That man would eat cranberries with everything if he had a choice. I don't know where that comes from, but he sure does love them!

Michael: He's always been that way. Mom used to say he'd put them on his oatmeal if she'd let him.

(Everyone thoroughly enjoys the salmon dinner, and after the dishes are all picked up and loaded in the dishwasher, it's time for pumpkin pie, ice cream and coffee. True Minnesotans never serve dessert without coffee. It's the unofficial state drink, just like the mosquito is the state bird. By seven o'clock, everyone has had it and is ready to walk across the street to the Lodge and go to bed. The last two to leave are Michael and Mark. Chuck notices Mark whispering something to his brother, and then Michael takes Mark's arm and leads him over to Carmelle, who is putting things away in the kitchen cupboard. She turns to Mark.)

Mark: (places his hand on Carmelle's shoulder) Thank you very much for the delicious, dinner, Mom.

Carmelle: (Tears form in her eyes, and she is glad Mark can't see them when he gives her a big hug.) It was my pleasure, Mark. I'm so glad Linda, William Francis and you were able to make the trip. (Carmelle and Mark embrace.) It's been a real joy for your dad and me to spend time with all of you.

Michael: (hugs Carmelle) You and Dad made it a joy for all of us! Thank you both for the wonderful dinner and for everything you did to make our trip special. It's been really great!

(With that the boys give their father a goodnight hug and head out the door to the Lodge. In the morning, everyone is rested, fed, and ready to head for the airport and home. It has been an action-packed visit, a pleasant, rewarding, love-filled time together, a trip everyone will remember, especially Chuck, who has been able to see his sons. After everyone has said their goodbyes, William Francis turns and sees his dad and Uncle Michael in a quiet corner with Grandpa Chuck. The two brothers give their father a big hug, but before Michael leads his brother away, Mark puts both hands on his father's face, his fingers holding it in a warm embrace.)

Mark: We love you, Dad!

NARRATOR: Carmelle and Chuck wait for the airplane to taxi down the runway and lift off before they head home. When Carmelle turns to Chuck and sees tears in his eyes, she knows what he is thinking, that he likely won't see his sons, his beloved "Twin Lights," ever again.)

ACT V:
THE FINAL MEETING

Scene I: The Downward Spiral – Carmelle's Dementia

NARRATOR: A couple of years after all of the relatives have left for Minnesota, Chuck notices that Carmelle is beginning to forget things, but he doesn't think anything of it because what ninety year old doesn't forget things? He certainly does! Then one day when Chuck goes to see his vascular surgeon, the doctor turns to him when he's leaving the examining room and asks, "Is Carmelle still with you?" Chuck begins wondering if the doctor knows something about Carmelle that he doesn't. He sure does. The downward spiral had begun.

Carmelle begins forgetting her purse in places like COSTCO when they're out shopping for groceries, and one day early in the morning she walks out of the house and is found by a neighbor sitting in the cab of his pickup truck. That's when something has to be done. Her son, Billy, installs chimes above each door that sound off if anyone leaves the house after bedtime. They work like a charm, even during the daytime when Chuck forgets to turn them off.

What puzzles Chuck is when Carmelle begins filling up grocery bags with her clothes and lining them up in the bedroom. He asks, "What are you doing putting all of these clothes in grocery bags, honey?" Carmelle answers, "I'm going home!" When Chuck hears those words, his heart sinks.

Near the end, Carmelle stops eating, and their general practitioner notifies the hospice agency about her condition. The agency provides a hospital bed and other equipment along with a hospice aide and hospice nurse to help Carmelle keep clean and comfortable at home.

Billy notifies the grandchildren, and they're sitting on the sofa cradling Carmelle when Father Miguel Grajeda comes to the house and gives her the rite of the sick and dying. It is what Carmelle would have wanted. Carmelle dies on January 23, 2023.

Scene II: The Funeral

NARRATOR: Carmelle's funeral is held at Santa Rosa Catholic Church in Cambria, California. Chuck reads the eulogy he composed about Carmelle's life.

Memories about Carmelle Dowdle

Chuck: Carmelle was born in a blizzard at Lockhardt, Minnesota on February 8, 1929. She said the doctor had to plow through a lot of snow to get to her, but he made it.

When Carmelle was a baby and all of the family and relatives were celebrating Thanksgiving, one of her aunts sat her down in a big bowl of warm mashed potatoes before they ate. I think Carmelle relished thinking about that scene.

Carmelle and her younger sister, Darlene, always chased around together. One of their favorite pastimes was to play at the grain elevator where their father, Elmer Johnson, worked. The girls would ride cups of grain to the top and then jump off before they were dumped in with the grain. Umm humm!

One hot summer day, Carmelle and Darlene went to the small grocery store where their mother had a charge account, and Carmelle wrote a note saying her mother wanted a pint of ice cream. The girls sat and ate the whole pint before they went home for dinner. When their father found out, they didn't get dinner, but their mother, Josephine, who loved her daughters dearly, brought them something to eat that evening anyway.

When Carmelle was 11 and Darlene was 8, their parents drove them to Omaha, Nebraska to a boarding school where two of their aunts were nuns. They arrived one day, and their parents were gone the next morning for a whole year. Darlene would run away when they came with cod liver oil, and when they served food she didn't like, she just wouldn't eat it, regardless of how long they made her sit. That girl had a strong will! One day when a nun died, the girls got up at night and went into the room where the corpse lay. They examined it, lifting the arms, touching the head, etc. They were curious kids! When their parents came to pick them up at the end of the school year, Carmelle told me Darlene and she had both learned a lot about life, good manners, and from their studies, and they both learned to speak Czech.

Carmelle's mother, Josephine Lutovsky, was Czech, and the four daughters would have done anything to please her. Besides English and Czech, Carmelle also spoke Spanish and other languages. She was multilingual, but wouldn't broadcast it. I once heard her speaking a foreign language (I didn't recognize) to a woman when we were going from the airport into London. That convinced me of her facility with languages.

Carmelle's mother wasn't satisfied with the small public school Carmelle started attending in the ninth grade, so she told her husband, Elmer Johnson, to get a job in Crookston, Minnesota, a nearby town of 7,000 people. Elmer got a job as a grain buyer at an elevator, and when the Johnsons moved to Crookston, Carmelle started ninth grade with me at Cathedral High School.

I don't think I ever spoke to Carmelle during all of my high school years, but my first wife, Marilyn Kirkwood, sure did. They were the two brightest women in our 1946 graduating class at Cathedral, and they became lifelong friends.

After graduating from Cathedral High School, Carmelle trained to become a nurse at St. Mary's Hospital, which was across the street from the Mayo clinic at Rochester, Minnesota. Carmelle worked as a nurse in Crookston for a short while and then went to Los Angeles where she met and married William Henry Matthes II. They moved to Sanger, California where they began raising a family and where Carmelle continued her nursing career.

The Matthes's had four children: Nancy, the eldest, became an attorney and died of cancer at a young age; Cathy is a University of California graduate and an artist; our friend, Bill Matthes, who learned to be a bricklayer from his dad, and who has built houses and is now a real estate broker in Cambria, and last, Johnny, the youngest.

Carmelle was a lovely woman, beautiful and bright, a no nonsense kind of gal. When her grandson-in-law graduated as a physician's assistant and wanted to celebrate by going skydiving and nobody would do it with him, Grandma Carmelle at 70 volunteered! It made the local papers, and Carmelle described what it was like walking out on the wing of a small airplane before jumping. That woman was fearless!

After our spouses died, I visited friends in Tustin and a cousin in San Diego and also stopped to see Carmelle. I was ecstatic when I left her and could hardly wait to come back and see her again, sooner rather than later, and did! We were married on April 21, 2001. I loved Carmelle and always will, forever!

Carmelle was well traveled before she met me and was always full of surprises. She had been to Prague, Czechoslovakia to visit with relatives and to Russia and other countries. One day I came home and Carmelle said, "We're going to China for three weeks and to Thailand for a week. I already bought the tickets." I just about lost my eyeteeth when she said that, but it sure was the adventure of a lifetime for me, and that was just the beginning of our travels together. Now she's traveled alone to her God, and I can just hear her saying, "**I love You!**" when she meets **Him** face to face.

Scene III: Planning

Chuck: I recently read an article written by Abbot Douglas Mullin, O.S.B. in the Spring 2024 issue of the *Abbey Banner Magazine*, and I think it applies to all of us. Before he was asked to accept the abbatial election at Saint John's Abbey in Collegeville, Minnesota, Abbot Mullin was chaplain at the Saint Cloud, Minnesota VA, a job he had planned to be his "retirement career." When he was elected abbot of St. John's Abbey, his retirement plans changed dramatically. I'd like to share with you the first two paragraphs of what Abbot Douglas Mullin had to say about "Planning."

"Planning is a good idea. Individuals, organizations and societies create plans to serve as a roadmap for accomplishing those things deemed important. When we plan, we identify goals and strategies to accomplish those goals. Good planning clarifies one's sense of purpose and direction. Lack of planning or poor planning can leave people floundering or feeling helpless.

And yet, planning has its limitations. A primary limitation lies in the planners' inability to anticipate all variables and uncertainties. It's impossible to foresee every possible outcome or obstacle. To be sure, I believe that the variables and uncertainties are the context through which God often interacts with us, calling us to trust in Divine Providence. As a result, good plans need to be flexible so they can be adapted, adjusted, or revised in response to changing circumstances."

I think Abbot Douglas Mullin, O.S.B. hit the nail right on the head:

1. Marty and I didn't plan on Michael and Mark being born early, and they didn't plan on Mark being blind, but they adjusted.

2. Linda and Laurie didn't plan on getting pregnant, and when they did, Laurie didn't plan on Gretchen having Down syndrome, but they adjusted.
3. Linda, Mark and Michael didn't plan on having to drop out of grad school the first year at the University of Minnesota, but they adjusted.

NARRATOR: Now, Chuck, with Carmelle's untimely death from complications of dementia, has to make adjustments, too. He reads an article in the *New York Times* titled, "Loneliness Shapes Our Behaviors and Perhaps Our Brains," and he responds to the article with this Letter to the Editor:

Dear Editor,

Certainly "loneliness" is a problem that can have devastating effects on humans' behavior and humans' brains, but "engineered social situations and cognitive behavioral therapy" aren't always successful for a reason. Something is missing! We're physical, emotional, mental, and spiritual animals. As a Christian, if I lack physical, emotional, mental, and/or spiritual support from my community, I can always rely on God, Jesus Christ, and the Blessed Virgin, who are my Father, Brother, and Mother, for support and friendship.

—Chuck Dowdle

Nowadays, whenever Chuck meets someone when he's walking on the boardwalk at the Fiscalini Ranch Preserve by the ocean in Cambria, the first thing he says to them is, "You're talking to a twice blest man!" And then he tells them why. "I say this because I had the good fortune to be married to two beautiful, caring and loving women, Marty for 49 years before she died of ovarian cancer and Carmelle for 22 years before she died of complications of dementia." When he leaves whomever he's been talking with he usually calls out, "I sing the praises of women, all women!

I Am Because You Are

Acknowledgements

I'd like to acknowledge Linda Rumney, who is the mother of a Down syndrome daughter. Linda is also the daughter of Marge and Bill Wegner, who were two of Marty and my best friends. Thank you, Linda.

Lisa Saybe, a nurse and Dent, Minnesota resident, was an inspiration. Lisa read the rough draft and encouraged me to complete it. Lisa is herself a twin, and she is the mother of two sets of twins. Lisa is also the daughter of Jerry Knudson, who was one of my closest Crookston, Minnesota friends. Thank you, Lisa.

Made in the USA
Las Vegas, NV
08 January 2025

16058123R00135